Lost but Making Excellent Time

Lost but Making Excellent Time

Transforming the Rat Race into a Pilgrimage

JODY SEYMOUR

RESOURCE *Publications* · Eugene, Oregon

LOST BUT MAKING EXCELLENT TIME
Transforming the Rat Race into a Pilgrimage

Resource Publications
A division of Wipf and Stock Publishers
199 W. 8th Ave., Suite 3
Eugene, OR 97401

www.wipfandstock.com

ISBN 13: 978-1-60608-286-7

Manufactured in the U.S.A.

Dedicated to

The Congregation and Staff of Davidson United Methodist Church
"My dear Flock"
and to
Betty White, my spiritual guide
with appreciation to Cherry Stevens
for her work on the manuscript

Contents

Introduction / *xi*

1　In a Hurry to Find God / 1

2　Monkeys, Minds, and Sunsets / 4

3　You Are Here / 7

4　The Christian Year: A Guide for Not Getting Lost / 9

5　Advent: Beginning Again / 12

6　Advent / 17

7　What in the World Are We Waiting For? / 18

8　Advent Waiting / 20

9　Prepare: A Poem for Advent / 21

10　Between Two Worlds / 22

11　Christmas: The Season of the Kidnapped Child / 23

12　How to Find the Baby / 25

13　Christmas Does Not Matter / 28

14　No Room / 30

15　A Manger Scene or Dirty Diapers? / 32

16　Still Christmas / 34

17　Manger Message / 35

18　Everybody but Jesus / 37

19 And a Little Child Shall Lead Them / 39

20 Mother Mary's Thoughts / 42

21 Poem for Christmas / 43

22 Swaddling Clothes / 44

23 Time for Christmas / 47

24 To Listen / 48

25 Epiphany: Sunshine on a Cloudy Day / 49

26 Light in the Darkness / 52

27 Distant Star / 54

28 Standing in Line / 55

29 Lent: The Necessary Wilderness / 57

30 Ash Wednesday: Branded with a Cross / 60

31 Dream Dust / 62

32 It's Not Supposed to Be Easy / 64

33 These Hands / 66

34 Some Other Way / 67

35 Holy Week: The Cost of Love / 68

36 Father Your Shoes Are Hard to Fill / 70

37 Hide Me / 73

38 Say Something / 75

39 Eulogy for Jesus / Pieta / 78

40 Easter: Empty Promises / 83

41 So Empty / 87

42 A Stranger on the Road / 89

43 Telling Resurrection / 90

44 Pentecost: A Really Good Ghost Story / 92

45 Sun Dried Tomatoes / 95

46 Thirsty / 97

47 Recall Jesus? / 98

48 How Far from Heaven / 100

49 Imago Dei / 102

50 A Prodigal Kind of Love / 103

51 God's Front Porch / 105

52 Ephphatha / 107

53 Creation / 108

54 Caught to Catch / 111

55 As Close as Your Next Breath / 112

56 The Forgetting / 114

57 The Shepherd's Valley / 116

58 The Work of Doing Nothing / 118

59 Beginning Again / 120

Appendix One—Preaching What I Practice: A Sermon for All
    Seasons / 123

Appendix Two—Advent: Making New Year's Resolutions at the End
    of Time / 124

Appendix Three—A Christmas Sermon: What Kind of Jesus Are You
    Expecting? / 129

Appendix Four—A Christmas Monologue Sermon: "The Adopted
Father" / 135

Appendix Five—Epiphany: The Baptism of the Lord / 143

Appendix Six—Transfiguration: God's Extreme Makeover / 148

Appendix Seven—Lent: Which Part is Yours? / 154

Appendix Eight—Christ the King Sunday: The Kingdom of God
/ 159

Appendix Nine—Pentecost Sunday: Passionate Kisses or a
Lukewarm Handshake / 163

Appendix Ten—Be Still and Know / 168

Appendix Eleven—Careful . . . There Really Is a Dark Side / 174

Appendix Twelve—Faith Healing or Healing Faith? / 180

Appendix Thirteen—Families, Children, and Teenagers / 185

Bibliography / 193

Introduction

IT IS AN OLD joke but its haunting punch line echoes the theme of our age. An air plane pilot announces to the passengers over the intercom; "Ladies and gentlemen I have some good news and some bad news. The bad news is that at this time I have no idea where we are. We seem to be completely lost. The good news is that we are making excellent time."

Every time I tell this joke as I prepare to teach or speak I get a "small" laugh. It is not really that funny but somehow its words penetrate the veneer of our culture. Most of us identify with the idea of being lost but making excellent time.

Perhaps the epitome of the pace of our culture is wrapped up in the scene I witnessed one day while driving in a large city. As I pulled to yet another stop in a long line of traffic I could feel and hear the beat of a radio playing in the car next to me. I turned toward the sound and saw a woman behind the wheel who was attempting to put on some lipstick with one hand while talking on her cell phone with the other hand. She leaned on the steering wheel with the hand that was struggling to apply the lipstick while looking upward toward the mirror on the sun visor.

In the seat beside her was a teenager with headphones on who was obviously not listening to the music that was on the car radio. Behind the teenager was a younger child also with headphones on and who held some kind of portable video game. She was pushing and bouncing either to the music or to her attempts at mastering the various motions needed to "win" on the small computer screen.

Within this microcosm of culture there was being played out what Richard Restak calls the sensory overload of our lives. In his book, "The New Brain: How the Modern Age is Rewiring Your Mind," Restak states that the demands of modern life divide attention so much that it effectively induces ADD.[1] In other words we are lost while making excellent time.

1. Restak, *The New Brain*, 46.

Restak states that sensory overload explains a lot of things, such as the fatigue people feel. Such analysis combined with research coming from Harvard Medical school by Gregg Jacobs in his work entitled "The Ancestral Mind" suggests that we are doing ourselves in with our over stimulation. Jacobs believes that the older "emotional" mind is being disconnected by overuse of the "thinking mind."[2]

These researchers believe that we must find ways and places to rediscover silence and to reestablish the balance between the rational and the emotional brains. In other words our original "wiring" is not meant to take in as much as we are taking in. The fact that we "can" take it in and seem to function well does not mean that we should take it all in.

With our technological "aids" we can "go fast" and that may seem like good news. The bad news is that we can get lost going so fast. As the old expression says, "When you get there where will you be?"

That car beside me in the midst of clogged traffic that seemed to be going nowhere represented for me a life too full. The wisdom teacher who poured tea into a cup for his waiting disciple is the story of our age. The disciple came to the wise teacher begging to be taught. The master first poured tea to the surprise of the would be student. The master kept pouring the tea until the cup was full and overflowing onto the floor.

The master kept pouring the tea into the full cup until the student shouted, "Master, stop the cup cannot contain any more." The master looked at the student and said, "And neither can you my child. You are too full. Go and empty yourself and then come back to me that I may give you some new wisdom."

In the pages that follow I want to look at some ways that we get lost while making excellent time. There will also be some suggestions for ways to slow down. I will use the structure of the Christian year as a guide or a map for the person who wishes to be a pilgrim on the journey of life rather than a tourist.

For the Christian who chooses to be a pilgrim, the year is patterned as a journey. On this journey there are places to acknowledge the "wilderness" areas rather than rush by them. There are places on the map of the Christian year to celebrate and to mourn. There are moments when the chance to "run and not grow weary" is offered as well as stops where the pilgrim is offered the opportunity "to come and die."

2. Jacobs, *The Ancestral Mind*, 9.

I am not sure we can avoid the traffic of life but we can keep from getting lost. Making excellent time is not the goal of the one who desires to be a pilgrim. And even for the technological tourist who hurries along, the question needs to be asked, "When you get there where will you be?"

Come slow down with me. We do not even have to "get there." I believe all of Jesus' words can be summed up in one expression, "Pay attention." The following words are offered to help us pay attention even if we do not make excellent time. Jesus offers words of wisdom to those who realize that they are "lost," even if they are making excellent time.

1

In a Hurry to Find God

WHILE WE ARE ON the subject of "being in a hurry" let's get to the subject of God. Our culture seems to act as if we "have" God. I hear talking heads on TV and on the radio proclaim that they have "spoken" with God and in so doing have all sorts of things to share with the rest of us. This often times includes sending in money so that "the conversation can go on."

Perhaps this subject of God sheds light on the core of our problem when it comes to "getting lost while making excellent time." In our hurry and insistence that we must "find" something when we search, we decide that we must find God. What we fail to consider is that the real "journey" that leads one to the divine is not as one-dimensional as our modern culture wishes it to be.

We think we "know" so much because we are a people who have discovered so much. I think we have been done in by *Google*. Oh, I have no beef with *Google*. I use the search engine all the time. But we think we can *google* God. We want God and the knowledge of God at our fingertips or at the beck and call of a mouse click.

Who do we think we are dealing with here? In our hurry to "find God" the real God must either laugh at us or be kind of upset with us.

The last time I checked we have recently "discovered" with the help of the Hubble space telescope that there are somewhere between 100 billion and 200 billion galaxies "out there," give or take a few billion. These galaxies are rushing away from each other at a rather alarming speed, which means that things are "still expanding" from what seems to have been a "big bang" some 14 billion years ago. And we think we can "have" the God who did all this because we "know" so much.

What we often do in order to "have" God is reduce God to manageable proportions. The problem is that this reduction may work for our fast paced need to know but what we get at the end of our search is not God. What we get are various forms of idol worship.

God becomes "the man upstairs" or our "co-pilot," or perhaps even our "buddy." Someone needs to rediscover one of the main themes of the Hebrew Scriptures in which the real God will have none of this. The real God does manage to incarnate the divine into the person of Jesus but just because we can sing, "What a Friend We Have in Jesus" does mean that we can get our hands around the power that creates galaxies that we are still discovering.

The story that may sum all of this up is found in Exodus 33:12–23 when Moses, who needs some instant credibility in order to work with the rabble slaves he is trying to lead, asks God to "see God's face." This is old language that says, "I want to understand your ways. I need to get a handle on you. I want *You*."

The ground shakes a bit and God "says" to Moses, "Moses I'll tell you what I will do. I will give you my deep abiding presence, but my face you cannot see." In other words, "I am the real God not the one you can put on your shelf or the one you can view on your TV screen. I am rather the God who is just beyond your ability to completely know."

Moses is then quickly hidden in the "cleft of the rock" and the real God passes by and do you know what Moses "sees?" Moses sees "God's coat-tails." If Moses, the main man of the Hebrew Scriptures, only gets a glimpse of "God Almighty," what do you and I think we get to "see"? Well if you listen to some pundits of the religious cause we can see and have most all of God. The problem is that in our hurry to "have" God we do not realize that we have "lost" the God of the universe and substituted one that is . . . well, manageable.

The real God is the God of the book of Job who says to a questioning Job, "Well, Job I'll show up and answer your questions but first answer me this. Where were you when I flung out into space those billions of galaxies? When was the last time you made a butterfly? Come on answer me and I'll answer you."

Who the heck do we think we are? Here is the way I see it. The FDA requires that labels on food products contain the ingredients according to the amount of the ingredients contained in the product. In other words what is most "in" the product has to be the first ingredient listed and then the rest are listed according to the amount contained within the product.

So, if you pick up a bottle that says, "fruit juice drink" but the first three ingredients listed on the label are "sugar, corn syrup, and artificial color" you can be sure that the word "fruit" is way down at the end of the list. You do not have the "real" thing.

What is the first "ingredient" on the label for the real God? I believe it is "mystery." Further down the list are such things as love and providence but if it is the real God of the universe who brought life from the past and who is still creating stars and black holes then we are dealing with a good deal of mystery.

I heard Alan Jones say in one of his lectures, "The opposite of faith is not doubt it is certainty." In our longing "to get there" and in our need "to know in a hurry" we figure out God but we get lost in so doing. The real God is full of mystery. It takes faith to stand in the "face" of such mystery and to be able to say, "I do not 'know' but I still believe."

Then what can be "known" about the real God? First of all if we are dealing with the real God and not the one we long to manage, we must slow down. The divine cannot be microwaved or packaged. Silence is the best and first response to prepare for a "glimpse" of the God of creation. Waiting upon God is the bedrock of knowing God.

God is not at the end of the cell phone call. God cannot be *googled*. We are not dealing with something we can load on an iPod.

Breathing can be medically described but it seems a mystery if you but pause. We breathe without thought. Breath is our starting point. To "know" God begins with slow, deep breaths. If we "run" to the burning bush we will be both out of breath and if we are not careful we might just pass it by in our hurry.

We must "take off our shoes," which means we must not run. We need to walk slowly and take deep breaths. The word for "spirit" in the scriptures is the same word for breath and wind. The religious quest for the real God is not a race. It is a walk and a pilgrimage. And at the end do not expect to "see the man behind the curtain." "My face you cannot see" God still whispers, "But if you slow down and breathe I will share with you a glimpse and you will 'know' my abiding presence."

2

Monkeys, Minds, and Sunsets

In her book, "The New American Spirituality" Elizabeth Lesser writes of being on an island where each evening one could view marvelous sunsets. There was one problem, the monkeys.

It seems that the best place to observe the sunset was at the end of the island where there was a grove of trees. As the sun would start to set many of the monkeys on the island would climb high into the grove of trees. Just as the shining orb was sinking below the horizon the monkeys would start a kind of chatter that was almost deafening. Somehow the setting sun, "set them off" into the realm of a noisy ritual that only the monkeys seemed to understand.

They would jump from limb to limb and start their song-like chatter just as the sun slipped beneath the ocean. Elizabeth seemed to not be able to refrain from looking to the trees to see this rather bazaar but captivating scene.

The problem was that in order to see the monkeys and their ritual she would have to turn in such a way as to not view the sunset. By the time she turned away from the monkeys, the beautiful sunset was gone.

On one evening as she found herself at her usual place to watch the sun take its leave she heard the monkeys behind her. Just as she started her almost hypnotic turn she stopped. With the monkeys doing their usual chattering behind her she writes, "I decided to watch the glorious sunset and let the monkeys be."[1]

I started to use this line as the title for this book. In our fast paced life where we get lost while making excellent time we have to decide if we are going to pay attention to the monkeys or the sunsets.

1. Lesser, *The New American Spirituality*, 142.

In Buddhism the lack of a centered mind is termed, "monkey mind." One of the goals of this ancient religion is to offer to "monkey mind" the quality of "mindfulness."

In the book, "The Pleasure Prescription" Paul Pearsall makes a differentiation between the brain and the mind. Our brains perform functions while our minds ponder depth. The problem of our culture seems to be that "our brain has lost its mind."[2]

We are "learning so fast" that we no longer "know." We leap from limb to limb making all sorts of noise but we miss too many sunsets

In his book, "The Culturally Savvy Christian" Dick Staub writes that we now live in a setting where, "Technology allows constant connectivity to our diversionary, mindless, celebrity driven popular culture" that offers "a soul numbing content around the clock."[3]

Our brains have lost their minds but we are making excellent time. I think it is worse than it used to be because of the over stimulation that our culture constantly offers us but this phenomenon is nothing new.

This "not paying attention" problem comes up one day when Jesus is walking through a field of wild flowers and his disciples are "lost" in conversation about maybe "which of them would be the greatest." Jesus makes them stop and probably has them sit down in the middle of the flowers.

In my mind's eye Jesus picks one of the flowers that is growing in the field and says, "Look at this flower." The word he uses is "consider the lilies." In his language the word means to "ponder with great attention." Those who are going to be the ones who are to continue in his "way" are missing too many sunsets and too many flowers on their hurry to "get somewhere."

Jesus probably knows that his disciples are headed toward becoming plumbers instead of water bearers. Okay, I know I've switched images again and that I am in danger of becoming a monkey in the grove of images but stay with me on this one.

Religion is the plumbing that carries the water. The water is the spirit of the living God but if we are not careful we end up worshiping the pipes and discover that we are still quite thirsty. Jesus does not mean for us to be plumbers tending pipes. He knows that pipes, "rust and become corrupted" like all the other "stuff" of the world.

2. Pearsall, *The Pleasure Principal*, 28.
3. Staub, *The Culturally Savvy Christian*, 15.

The authentic purpose of religion is to get water to the thirsty spirit. That is the reason that one must sit by the "well" and sometimes slowly draw the water rather than being consumed with making sure that the water is contained in a system of pipes somewhere so that it can rush along to the next place.

Throughout history and again in our present time, religion ends up being the cause of great suffering. People are now screaming out the name of God as they blow themselves and others up in the name of "religion." Some very misguided "plumbers" corrupt their religion causing many people to end up all the more thirsty.

It took a while for those disciples of Jesus to learn to "ponder." In the Gospel of John, a woman whom Jesus encounters by a well one noonday figures it out long before the disciples do. She ends up saying to Jesus, "Give me this water you speak of that I might not have to come to this well so often." All those around her, including Jesus' disciples, think that she should "get lost" because most of them are "worshiping the pipes" and do not understand the man who is offering "spiritual water." We still need to stop by the well and sit a spell before we hurry off to check out the plumbing. And while we are sitting at the well we need to not pay so much attention to all the "monkeys" over our shoulder. There are just so many sunsets.

3

You Are Here

IMAGINE YOU ARE STANDING in front on one of those signs in a large building or shopping mall with a directory or display indicating where you are. Usually a large "X" marks a spot with words beside the X reading, "You are here."

Where is the X for you? Every journey must begin somewhere so put an X beside you and let's start here. There is not much gained by analyzing how you got here but my suggestion is that many of us got "here" in excellent time but we may be a little lost.

I remember seeing a cartoon in which the outline of a whale was drawn with an X in the middle of the whale. Beside the X where the famous words, "You are here." The only caption for the drawing was the name *Jonah*.

Jonah is in a hurry to get to anywhere but where God wants him to go. Somewhere on his stormy escape he gets lost and finds himself consumed by the darkness. The "belly of the whale" may be a good image to describe where the pace of modern life often leads us.

It is like we have been swallowed by modernity and its sea of consumerism. We are not even aware that our surroundings are in fact not where we need to be or should be. We are being carried along by something bigger than we are but we are unaware of the motion because we seem to be standing still, relative to the X.

I don't mean to bleed this whale thing until it turns belly up but I think we are simply too available to most everything but the very thing we ought to be available to. The human spirit is being used up by overstimulation. We are too busy being busy. We are preoccupied with accessibility.

Cell phones, e-mails, and laptops on the beach are signs of this accessibility. We are so accessible that we are out of reach to the simple wonder of life and its rhythms. The spirit within us is surrounded by a consuming spirit of the age.

So for now, "You are here." "Here" is the only place you need to be. Read what is ahead "slowly." You do not have to get "there," wherever there is. It may have been Augustine who said, "Thou art the journey and the journey's end." If that is the case all of life is a pilgrimage and it is the journey that is important not the arrival. On this journey we do not have to "make excellent time."

You are here.

4

The Christian Year: A Guide for Not Getting Lost

I AM USING THE Christian calendar in this book to help us slow down and pay attention. The Christian year is obviously not in accord with the calendars and "Blackberries" that we use to shape our days. This is as it should be because the Christian calendar is meant to be an "alternate" guide.

We all know how the calendars on our desks and refrigerators shape our lives or perhaps misshape our lives. Perhaps the "old" Christian calendar with its "different" way of measuring time can help us find "another way." This way of marking time that we now call the Christian calendar is modeled after the Hebrew way of measuring time. This way of measuring can be more like a compass than a clock. The Christian calendar can help us not just mark time but can aid us in giving meaning and direction to time.

We know that Christian calendars were being used as early as the third or fourth centuries but they were based on the religious heritage found in Leviticus 13. The Hebrew people know that God called them to de different and not like "all the nations around you."

How then are they to be "different"? Their distinctiveness is to be found in the covenants that they keep that are originated by the God who calls them to be "set apart." These sacred promises lead the people to "mark" time in a different way than the nations around them.

Festivals like the Passover and Festival of Weeks are originated based on agriculture and animal habits. The reason for this is not simply because the Hebrew peopled raise animals and crops but because these animals and crops are an intricate part of the sacrificial system that ties the people to their allegiance to their God.

It is no wonder that when the "new Israel" is forming itself and its identity it too looks to an alternative way of measuring time. The "people of the way" who come to be known as Christians look to their past religious heritage to form the new "calendar."

The first change that is to be "new" is that the traditional "Sabbath" day is transferred to Sunday because this was the day of the Lord's resurrection and the first day of the week. The Christians know that they must distinguish themselves even from their former standing in the religion from which they come.

As the Christian calendar develops over the centuries the old pattern of festivals can be seen as the background for the new way of measuring time. The first "cycle" of the Christian year is based on Passover and becomes the Easter cycle. The season of preparation for this celebration of the Passover of death in Jesus' resurrection becomes the season of Lent. Since the Jewish people are accustomed to Pentecost as the celebration of the harvest and the giving of the Law, the "new" Christians use this model to celebrate the "giving of the spirit" and the need to "go into the fields" and harvest disciples. At a later time the season after Pentecost comes to be known as "ordinary time" which means to "mark the days." This lengthy season is sometimes divided into Pentecost and Kingdomtide and emphasizes the "work of the Kingdom."

The next "season" that is formed centers on the birth of Jesus. In this cycle the Christians form their own pattern with what we now know as the season of Epiphany. In the formation of the early Christian community Epiphany marks the celebration not only of Jesus' birth but also the coming of the Magi, the remembrance of Jesus' baptism, and his first miracle at Cana.

A bit later the nativity becomes more important and a separate season is set aside that we now call Christmas. Since there is a time of "preparation" for Easter there arises a time of preparation for Christmas that we now know as Advent.

So we have a "different" calendar from the "world's" calendar. This can be an opportunity to take an old custom and let it become new for those of us who "get lost while making excellent time." Paying attention to a different way of measuring our days can help us be "in the world but not of the world."

The thoughts and suggestions that now follow are presented so that we can together find an alternate way of measuring time. The calendars that we hang from our refrigerators or mark up on our desks can help us keep appointments. We also need a way to mark time that reminds us that we are not just people on a "trip" through life but we are rather "pilgrims on a journey." The Christian year offers times that call to mind the inward journey and the need to nourish the spirit.

5

Advent: Beginning Again

Steven Covey, in his book "First Things First" makes the distinction between living life by a compass or a clock. Herein is part of the way we get lost while making excellent time.[1]

One old expression says, "When you get there where will you be?" Our age is like the fable of the tortoise and the hare. We need to remember who "gets there" and who "wins." It is not the fast paced rabbit. He gets lost even though he thinks he is making excellent time.

That "wise sage," Jimmy Buffet reminds us of a different view of time:

> I bought a cheap watch from a crazy man floating down Canal
> It doesn't have numbers or moving hands, it always just says now.
> Now you may thinking that I was had,
>   but this watch is never wrong,
> And if I have trouble the warranty said,
> Breathe in, breathe out, move on.
> According to my watch, the time is now,
> The past is dead and gone.
> Don't try to shake it, just nod your head,
> Breathe in, breathe out, move on.[2]

A more poetic way of expressing this coming to oneself by slowing down is expressed in T. S. Elliot's "The Four Quartets"

---

1. Covey, *First Things First*, 2.

2. Buffett, "Breathe in, Breathe Out, Move On." *Take the Weather with You*. RCA, 2006.

We shall not cease from exploration and the end of all our exploring will be to arrive where we started and know it for the first time.[3]

Like some "wild hare" we often run by the place where we started so we cannot know it. We need a new old beginning to remind us of starting places.

Advent is a new old beginning. The word "Advent" means, "coming." Advent is a reminder that life is never "done" it is always coming.

The yearly calendar marks time in segments of doing. This marking of time is akin to a clock. The Christian calendar is more about "being" and has to do with the inner journey that leads to a beginning that needs a compass rather than a clock.

The Christian calendar begins in the wilderness and asks of the pilgrim, "Who do you want to be?" The "world's calendar" seems to ask of us, "Where do you want to go?"

As Advent begins, an ascetic prophet lines people up in the wilderness and screams at them to "get clean" before it is too late. He sounds strangely like an "end of the world" doomsday kind of guy. John the Baptist tells everybody in line that the ax is being laid to the root of the tree and that the grain is being sifted. What is not found to be unacceptable will be burned in the unquenchable fire.

This does not sound like such a good way to "begin" but this is no ordinary way to mark time. This beginning "begins" with the assumption that we start out "lost," and need to be found. If we are indeed "lost" while making excellent time this is a good way to begin.

In the movie, "Forest Gump" Forrest tells the lady sitting beside him on a park bench, "And I met the Pres-I-dent of the United States, A-gain." This low IQ pilgrim tells his life story, which includes both unbelievable bad times and undeserved good times, but he ends up meeting three different presidents so he simply says the last time he meets one of the Presidents that he met the President "a-gain."

The Christian year begins each year "a-gain" in the wilderness. Life seems full of wilderness experiences. If we are going to come back to place we started and "know" it for the first time this is a good place to begin?

Each Advent the assigned scriptures of the Christian year tell of the stars falling from the sky and the moon not giving its light. This is

3. Elliot, *The Four Quartets*, V.

no, "high self esteem let's all feel good" way of marking time. Christian Smith calls what often passes for the Christian faith these days a form of Moralistic Therapeutic Deism.

This brand of faith is not about spiritual disciplines and discovering the depth of religious tradition. This twisting of faith ends up espousing a God of distance who is only invited in when something needs fixing. Its aim is to make one feel good and fulfilled. There is a general "feeling" of morality that has something to do with being nice to each other, but there is no room for either sacrifice for the good of social justice nor is there a place for repentance because there is no sin.[4]

Advent begins with recognition of "sin." This recognition of an old fashioned word is far removed from any form of Moralistic Therapeutic Deism. Advent begins with the wilderness. The "season" begins with a person standing in line to be baptized who is not in need of getting cleaned up. When John recognizes Jesus, John goes into a kind of "You gotta be kidding" thing and refuses to do the deed. Jesus says, "Get over it John. I know what I am doing and you don't so baptize me and hush up."

Jesus knows where to begin. He wants to be "with" his people and help them begin to understand what the word "Emmanuel" really means. "God with us" is going to take on new meaning. Jesus then goes into the wilderness for 40 days or so to spend some time with the "dark side" of life. What does this say?

It says that this "beginning" takes the darkness seriously right from the beginning. The darkness is powerful. A feel good kind of religion has its place but it is not suitable in this beginning. Jesus slows down the pace from the start. He takes a journey of self-discovery before he begins the "race."

All this is interesting in light of what we have done to Advent in America. We "do" Advent by not observing it. The season of Advent is often lost in the midst of the countdown of shopping days until Christmas. Advent ends up being only plumbing to convey the rushing waters of Christmas.

But in the Christian calendar this cannot happen. The blocks, the days, and the numbers cannot simply be ripped off all at once. Advent is itself a journey and is all about "waiting." Today we somehow do not

---

4. Smith, *Soul Searching: The Spiritual Lives of Teenagers*, 118.

want Mary to be pregnant. We want her to have the baby like it is some 30-minute TV show that has to end up happy and quick.

Advent is a pregnant time of waiting and it is a symbol of what the whole year is going to be. There is no way to make excellent time on the journey that lies ahead. Behind the scenes of the Christian calendar is the remembrance that those newly freed slaves from Pharaoh's Egypt have to learn a lesson in waiting. They want to take the expressway to the Promised Land only to discover that God makes them go around in circles for 40 or so years in order to find themselves.

It seems that this newly formed people of God "pass Go" and fail to collect what they need. They have to take a journey in order to discover the place from which they started and to know it for the first time.

So Advent is not only the beginning season of the Christian calendar it is also a window through which all of time is measured and marked. To stand in the baptismal waters of Advent with a dripping wet Jesus is to be reminded that the journey ahead is not going to be a race but a pilgrimage.

One way to experience this need to wait before starting a journey is to walk a labyrinth. Walking a labyrinth is an ancient form of prayer. A labyrinth, unlike a maze, does not have any dead ends. There is one way into the center and one way out.

The process of walking a labyrinth models the spiritual journey and gives the one who would be a pilgrim of life rather than a tourist a way to walk through life. The first thing the walker must do in walking a labyrinth is to be mindful. This means to be awake to what is going to happen.

I teach a personality system known as the Enneagram. The Enneagram model states that there are nine different "trances" in which people chose to live. These trances are often called personality types but behind the Enneagram theory is the premise that most of us sleep walk through life. We are robotic in our way of experiencing life and therefore miss much of what happens both within us and in our outer world.

This is why the breath prayer is one of the most ancient forms of prayer. To pay attention to one's breath makes a person present to him or herself. One way to get lost while making excellent time is to put our lives on "cruise control."

The first step of a mindful journey is to make sure we are awake. The next step as one walks the labyrinth is one of purgation. As the pilgrim walks toward the center of the labyrinth the opportunity is offered to strip away or let go of whatever is holding a person back. This is the beginning of a style of life that is built upon promise.

The ancient word *covenant* is based upon a word that means to cut. Hebrew covenants usually involve sacrifice and the cutting into an animal so that blood is shed to show the seriousness of this life-giving oath. To let go as one walks does not mean to "give up." Letting go helps the pilgrim not give up what is truly important but helps one delineate what is vital and what is not.

As one arrives at the center of the labyrinth the next step is ask for illumination. After the letting go of purgation, room is made for something new to be given from outside of oneself. Leonard Cohen offers the following thoughts:

> Ring the bells that still can ring,
> Forget your perfect offering
> There is a crack in everything,
> That's how the light gets in.[5]

As the pilgrim walks out of the labyrinth the request is for unity. Only after being awake, letting go, and the gift of new illumination can one receive something new. Often times in our fast paced culture we want illumination in a microwavable form. We do not want to wait, we are often sleep walking or are on cruise control, but we want to "get there" quick and find what we need when we get there.

The journey that begins at Advent is a journey that will need to be taken at a slower pace. It is a journey that will require that we go back to the beginning often and make sure we are awake. Like walking the labyrinth we end up at the place "from which we started" and hopefully know it for the first time.

---

5. Cohen, "Anthem." *The Essential Leonard Cohen*. Sony, 2002.

6

Advent

Endings in the wilderness—
A prophet scatters seeds
on desert sands
screaming that hope
will grow
amidst dry despair

Surprises amidst the impossible—
A frightened teenager hears
an angel proclamation
telling her of a coming
star child
through her to the world

Dreams that make no sense—
An eager Joseph longing for
children of his own
but hearing that his
first born
will not be his

Waiting yet again on wonder—
An old story told yet again
into a world of terror—
needing seeds of hope
an angel proclaims
a child
first born of God

Advent again…

7

What in the World Are We Waiting For?

I F I WAKE UP in eternity and there is a line in which I have to wait, I will know that I have missed the boat and heaven escapes me. Waiting is not my thing

So Advent as a season is a bit of a challenge. The surrounding landscape of our consumer culture conveniently forgets Advent because we have become a "no-waiting" society. Better than any Christmas carol is the voice over the intercom that announces, "No waiting at check-out 7."

Try convincing a seed to go to "checkout 7." One sure way to not have any fruit is to rush a seed's growth. Those "woolly worms" that crawl across the pavement predicting with their numbers of bands the coming of cold weather understand Advent better than we do. They have within their DNA the potential to wait.

Caterpillars are born with mystery in their fiber, which they use to spin a cocoon of pause. The magic of butterflies is but a dream to a woolly worm but the risk is part of their very being.

We who have forgotten how to crawl now manage to run through life. The "Christmas Rush" has become a mantra of acceptance of what must surely be. So what is more "real," the cycle of nature or the computer enhanced speed of our present thinking?

The season of Advent offers a sea wall that stands facing a tsunami of oncoming holiday expectations. Those who grieve, who are lost, or who are missing out on the "most wonderful season of all" seem to understand the strange wisdom of waiting. They have to wait.

So for them and for us Mary does not adopt baby Jesus. She does not get a phone call telling her to drop by some agency to pick up a child that suddenly is available. A very surprised Mary gets a visit from an angel telling her that if she is willing to wait upon the work of God within her, she will give birth to the long awaited Redeemer.

After nine months of waiting, and after waiting in line outside an inn only to be told that there is no room, Mary's waiting finally ends in a barn. Was it worth waiting for?

Somewhere in all the frantic nature of the season we need to find some time for waiting. If you are like me and waiting is not part of who you are, that is even better. The foolishness of God is supposed to challenge our "wisdom" at certain times.

Every year a prophet screams into the wilderness of Advent, "Prepare the Way of the Lord." John the Baptist's faith ancestor, Isaiah, says it this way,

> Those who wait upon the Lord shall renew their strength,
> They shall mount up with wings like eagles,
> They shall run and not grow weary,
> They shall walk and not faint. (Isaiah 40:31)

Maybe there will be a line outside eternity's door after all. It is worth waiting for.

8

Advent Waiting

Waiting—fingers slowly tracing
   love across the stretched flesh
   on an abdomen full of hope

Waiting—some nameless innkeeper
   ponders how angry travelers
   will find enough room

Waiting—shepherd's thoughts escape
   toward empty heavens soon
   to be full of angel voices.

Waiting—all Creation like some
   spinning cocoon filled with
   wings of anticipation.

Waiting—so must we
   on birth, and crowds, and common
   folk who announce God's surprise.

9

Prepare

A Poem for Advent

Again in some distant wilderness
    will come a warning cry,
        "Prepare the way!"
"My ways are not your ways,"
    shouts the God of this
        crusty desert prophet.
"One is coming whom you do not expect."
But we know what we want
    and we aim to find
        what we need,
So we are in danger of missing
    his distant warning of
        "Prepare."

Waiting has become a lost art form,
    for instant is our life
        of no preparation
We have plastic money to buy dreams
    that need no dreaming,
        for we can have dreams "now."
You are alone in your waiting wilderness, John.
We no longer have the time to pause
    and ponder manger mystery,
        since for us nativity is instant.
O prophet, shout into our too full ears
    that word we cannot buy,
        "Prepare!"

Between Two Worlds

Tinsel tossed and bubble lights
seem like moisture
that forms on the
inside of the window
of my soul—
only to fade away
as morning crests

Between the world of electric trains
that only went round
in small circles
and erector sets
that built
a simple world—
I now find myself

The manger scene, always on
the mantle witnessed
a world that quickly
passed away into
video games and
laptops whose knowledge
surpassed the old ways

And so I need this Advent
to help me between
my two worlds
where I sense a kind
of wilderness
where the child in me longs
again for a savior

Christmas: The Season of the Kidnapped Child

COULD THERE BE ANYTHING more horrible than a story of a child being kidnapped from the nursery while the parents are sleeping? Perhaps that is what happens at Christmas. We wake up amidst Christmas carols that begin near Halloween and decorations in stores that push out even the few turkeys that rush by at Thanksgiving.

The child is kidnapped by culture. Just as puzzled archeologists ask if there ever was a manger "out back," so we wonder what happens to the baby. Was he ever there? Is it a sweet dream too good to be true?

I remember Dean Cleland screaming out a sermon at Duke Chapel when I was in seminary proclaiming that there is no need to "put Christ back into Christmas" because he was never there to begin with. History shows that the holiday of Christmas seems devised by a Pope who was not about to have the Roman pagan ritual of Saturnalia out do the new Christian faith so we have Christmas on December 25.

Those who wish to ponder such things figure that Jesus was probably born in the springtime when shepherds would have had their sheep "out in the fields." Maybe the baby never had a chance. He was kidnapped early on by culture.

Dean Cleland urged his congregation that day to "give up on Christmas" and don't worry about putting Jesus back into something he was never in to begin with. "Enjoy your families, sing some carols, try to stay sane, and then 'observe' Christmas during the season of Epiphany," Cleland urged. Epiphany was probably the earliest date that the first Christians observed Jesus' birth before the Pope started putting out manger scenes in December.

It seems that for the very first Christians Jesus' birth was not so important. Mark the earliest gospel written does not record a birth story. Paul, the earliest record of any of the New Testament writings, does not mention wise men or mangers or "sore afraid" shepherds. What the earliest followers of Jesus seem spell bound by are not angel voices on still nights in Bethlehem but angry shouts of "crucify him" that come at the end of things.

Jesus' death and the why of it consumes early Christian thinking followed closely by the Resurrection accounts. His death precedes his birth in importance.

But what do those early Christians know? We have managed to elevate Christmas to new heights. The economy needs it even if early Christian pilgrims do not.

The old expression is to "keep" Christmas. I think it is worth trying. There is something very special about the nativity stories. Sure they spill over with legendary images and bare the makings of deep myth but he "was born" and I am all for returning the child to the nursery and shedding light on the kidnappers.

Since the theme of this whole book is that we get lost while making excellent time it should be no surprise that the baby easily gets "lost" in the Christmas rush. The themes of "no room," of a young pregnant and probably very fearful unmarried girl, the need for angel voices in a crazy world, and the willing search of wise men; are all images that can be very meaningful in this fast paced world.

Let's find the baby.

12

How to Find the Baby

THE FIRST WAY TO "find the baby" in the craziness of the season we call Christmas is to slow down and do what the grown up baby says is essential for spiritual development. One "dark" night Jesus says to a supposedly wise religious leader of the day, "You must be born again."

Nicodemus responds, "How can a person go back into the womb?" Jesus shakes his head and says something like, "I thought you were supposed to be a leader for others, Nick, and you do not even know the fundamentals. This is not about the birth of flesh and bones. This is about what is really important, the continual birth of soul and spirit."

John's gospel loves the image of light and dark to portray those who "get it and those who do not." Nick is "in the dark." He is all grown up with no place to go. Nick is a religious Humpty Dumpty who needs to fall or be knocked off the wall and break open. Jesus knows that for birth to happen there needs to be some slowing down and some letting go. The down and dirty way to say this is that Nick needs to "die" to something so that he can live for something.

Nick is the equivalent of the Rich Ruler who is wrapped too tight in his possessions to let go enough to follow Jesus. This wannabe disciple wants to follow Jesus but he wants to have everything stay the same in order to do it. I know how that feels.

My uncle Foster was the only member of my father's family who did not sell his shrimp boat and flee to the new shipyard in order to make a lot more money for a lot less hard work. Shrimping is risky business and those relatives of mine knew a good thing when they saw it.

It "cost" them their boat but they gained a new way of life. Foster did not want to let go of the old ways because he loved to come in early from shrimping and stop at the local watering hole beside the dock. He would arrive home later in the evening "two sheets in the wind" and offer all kinds of wisdom to those in the family who were foolish enough to turn away from the good life.

Foster did admit that he would like to have some of that good money that his brothers were now making but he did not want to let go of his boat and his ways. He discovered the same thing that Jesus' disciples discover when faced with the new ways that Jesus offers. Jesus comes up out of his baptismal waters and says, "Repent and believe the good news."

The word "repent" means to turn around and go in a different direction. Foster, like those first disciples, was a fisherman; but he wanted to repent but still keep his boat. Nicodemus comes to Jesus "at night" and is interested in trying on some of Jesus' teachings for size but all he need do is ask some of those disciples standing around Jesus that evening and Nick would discover like Foster discovered, "You cannot repent and keep the boat."

To recover the baby is to come face to face with the need in our lives to be "born again." The pace of Christmas will kidnap the child every year if we do not do something. Our progress and our pace are costly.

Mark Nepo in his book, "The Exquisite Risk," writes that we live in a "gap" created by the difference in what we know and what we know well. Our technology and our fast pace is a kind of science in which we "do" life. Nepo points out correctly that the word "science" comes from a Latin word that means, "to know." The word "conscience" on the other hand comes from a Latin word that means, "to know well."

Nepo writes:

> We characterize the ability to know as retaining information and the ability to know things well as internalizing what matters. The impact of technology has extended dramatically what it is we know at a much faster rate than our ability to know things well. For to know things well requires time. But the advent of phone wires and the microchip have thrust us into a life of incredible speed, where we retain much more than we can internalize.[1]

Nepo calls this "gap" between what we know and what we know well, the cost of progress. I call it "lost while making excellent time." As Nepo puts it, "As we retain more we internalize less." I agree with him when he writes:

---

1. Nepo, *The Exquisite Risk*, 84.

In our time on this earth, we are constantly bombarded with more to know and constantly faced with the challenge to slow things down in order to choose which of all this is essential to know well. At the end of each day, we are forced to ask: What is the one true thing of the many that we are shouted at to use? . . . In light of all this, we might understand inner practice as a daily way to glimpse Oneness and as a inner aerobic to compensate for the human cost of progress.[2]

Using Nepo's image Nicodemus comes at the "end of the day" and discovers that he will remain in the dark unless he is willing to be born again. Nick knows a lot but he does not know well. His "information" needs to be birthed into faith and his ability to accumulate religious truth needs to be "internalized" as insight that will make a difference in the way he lives. Nick is lost while making excellent time but he stands at the edge of new birth.

So to "find the baby" at Christmas will mean slowing down and doing some inventory of what we know well. In the cacophony of Christmas what is "the one true thing of the many" that stands as important and vital? If Jesus is right, in order to discover what that one true thing is, we will have to slow down and let go. Tending babies takes time and patience. No wonder we want to rush through Christmas.

It is still true; you cannot repent and still keep the boat. Progress ironically is filled with old, fast paced ways that will need to be bridled so that we can slow down enough to discover our true selves and glimpse the God within. Christmas is about new birth for people caught in old ways. The baby might have been kidnapped but he can be rediscovered at the edge of night somewhere between the thinking of Nicodemus and Foster.

Yes, Nick, you will have to fall off the wall and split open to see what is inside to discover the new birth. And no, Foster, you cannot repent and still keep the boat. Real Christmas has a cost to it and it is not found on the Visa card statement in January.

---

2. Ibid, 86.

13

Christmas Does Not Matter

Christmas does not matter
except to those
for whom
darkness seems a
shroud to be
worn forever

Christmas does not matter
except to children
who believe
that trust is like
a shredded
birth certificate

Christmas does not matter
except to broken hearts
that need
to know that deep
love is seeking
their healing

Christmas does not matter
except to a world
whose upside-down
priorities need to
be righted
yet another time

Christmas does not matter
except to God
whose manger child
longs always to be born
again and again
to people who
long to know
that with
the
Christ Child . . .
It always and forever
matters.

14

No Room

SLEEPING. WAS ALL THE world sleeping? Joseph, wrapped in a blanket with only his tired head showing, was beginning that rhythmic pattern of breathing that Mary had become familiar with in her short time with him. Even the cow, who had lost its manger to the necessities of the evening, seemed lost in night dreams.

And the child, having tasted the first nourishment this side of a starlight journey, lay sleeping at her breast. The world was sleeping.

In the silence she could hear echoes of distant memories. The announcement from the blinding light in her window seemed now to be reflected in a more than bright evening star. "You are blessed among all women," a voice from the light had proclaimed. Impossible had become something stirring within her for these months of waiting. Now she held the impossible sleeping in her arms.

The voice of her Joseph at first saying "no" and then holding her within a "yes" combined with the soft evening song of crickets. She began humming a lullaby whose words came to her in the many night dreams that held her in those months of waiting. Angels were in her dreams, and they always seemed to be singing. As she closed her eyes it seemed as if those angels were now singing into the silence of this evening of sleep:

> Sleep little Jesus, my dear little child,
> Angel's breath, so tender so mild
> Gift to the world, so much love you bring,
> Sleep little Jesus, to you I will sing.

She had whispered the song on other evenings in between her dreams. Now she sang it into reality and into the face of her mystery child.

What did this night mean? Why had there been no room? Tears filled her eyes. The entire world was sleeping. She was alone except for the one she held in her arms. Then deep within her came the words from a place between sleep and daydreams. Rocking him gently in her arms she added the new verse:

> Sleep little Jesus, no room in the inn,
> God's singing angels soon will begin,
> Telling the world, so all may now see
> That my little Jesus comes to set the world free.

Mary smiled at the new words. What wonders would come next? She looked into the face of the impossible and at last she joined a waiting world. She slept.

15

A Manger Scene or Dirty Diapers?

L ET'S FACE IT MANGER scenes are sweet. There is always a pensive Mary who looks nothing like a woman who has just been through not a sweet labor but a sweaty one. Joseph usually looks toward a smiling baby Jesus whose arms are often raised as if he is getting ready to reach up and take his first steps. This baby has no marks of birth on him and most of the time looks strangely like a combination of the "Gerber Baby" and one of those smiling perfect faces that makes us want to rush out and buy Pampers.

I like manger scenes. They are sweet and sweet is nice. The bitter taste of a war in the place where the traditional Garden of Eden was supposedly located and the ever-present threat of the next terrorist strike make one long for something sweet.

I wonder though if we need the reality behind the manger scene. Just after the frozen smile we see every Christmas on the infant Jesus there comes the moment when Mary or Joseph have to change a dirty diaper. Yes the child is real, and we need real more than we need sweet.

We need to know that God somehow enters our mess. That "fact" can be no more brought home than for us to remember that the Prince of Peace has diapers that need changing. What is more real than messy diapers?

Emmanuel is a wonderful sounding word and fits well in Christmas lyrics, but its meaning is, "God with us." God "is" with us in our mess. God is not watching in some frozen state like Joseph watching the child in our many different manger scenes. God is not simply a "sweet" concept and dream wish of a happy ending to a Christmas pageant. God is as real as a messy diaper because the original child needs "changing" as much as we need changing.

When you wrap up the manger scene this year stop a minute before you bundle up the baby. Someone changed his diaper. We are not alone. God is with us in the mess, really.

The kid outgrows his diapers, goes through adolescence, and the rest is history. When asked by some inquiring followers just where he can be "found" Jesus sys that he can always be discovered in the messes of life where people are broken, hungry, and held captive by life. He remembers messy diapers and so should we. Emmanuel, God is with us, really.

16

Still Christmas

Towers fall and poison fills
lives and promises death—
Still, Christmas stirs in the
ashes of buried dreams
and amidst another
desert the wind
scatters a shrill voice—
"Prepare!"
still . . . Christmas

Herod's in ages past and
today try to kill the truth—
Still, Christmas births itself
into waiting hearts
who long to know
that God will again
beckon voices in the stars to say,
"Behold!"
still . . . Christmas

17

Manger Message

Joseph, see it there
  as if it has been
      waiting
  all these years
  to be more than
  a feeding place

Shape the hay and
  make it his
      first bed—
  this manger's message
  will be told
  some day

For now, let him
  sleep in its
      cradling—
  these quite creatures
  watch as if
  they know

Hold him, manger
  as I have held
      him
  these months of
  waiting since my
  night of angel's voice

More than these simple
animals, the hungry
world
needs what you
hold this night
of divine mystery

Hold me Joseph, while
this manger holds
our child—
what will the world
do with this whisper
of God we offer?

18

Everybody but Jesus

GOING THROUGH BOXES OF possessions after her mother's death my wife Betsy discovered the manger scene she used as a child. It was packed away beneath a number of other items. As she unwrapped the small dusty figures she discovered, as she later said, "Everybody was fine but Jesus." The tiny haloed figure of baby Jesus was broken in pieces, some of which were not to be found.

> Your beginnings so broken
>   You reach up with but
>   one arm
> Did your manger not provide
>   that Christmas magic
>   so longed for by
>   those who call your name?

> We pack you away every season
>   Hoping to unwrap you
>   whole again
> But now even your haloed head
>   is torn from your
>   tiny molded frame
>   and you are broken.

> "Everybody was fine but Jesus,"
>   Says the one who found
>   the scene
> Shepherds stand by
>   and Wise Men still

kneel and offer gifts
ready for opening

You alone are found so wounded
    Sleeping disciples long ago
        packed you away
And those how would do you
    harm came and
    crushed your offered
    love on that tree

Did some angel look down and say,
    "Everybody did fine but Jesus?"
Because it is your brokenness
    that makes us whole
    and your shattered beginning
    reminds us of our own ends.

We can't even find your tiny legs
    You've gone missing again
Like that first time some
    came to say a final
    goodbye to your
    broken, forgotten body

Your father did what we cannot
    And pieced you back together
But for us and our weary
    souls you shall
    forever remain broken
    as you whisper again,
        "Take . . . it is broken for you."

19

And a Little Child Shall Lead Them

CHRISTMAS CONTAINS BOTH JOY and pain. The joy seems to always have something to do with childhood. Everyone has a childhood and even if Christmas does not produce everything our childhood longing desires there is at least the simplicity of anticipation that something good is coming. The pain comes from growing up and away from such childhood. We often spend our adult years shopping for children or grandchildren, in part as an effort to get back to the joy of childhood.

I reach back for that Christmas morning when our youngest child looked straight into my eyes at mattress level. She was just tall enough to look over the bed sheet and just old enough to discover new words daily.

The Christmas Eve pageant was still evidently looming in her young mind. After all she heard her father say at the end of the bath-robed drama that, "Tonight is the eve of Jesus' birth." Later that evening Santa made an early appearance at the "hut" out behind the small Sanctuary of the rural church I was serving.

Since the Santa and the Jesus thing were new to our two year old her mother and I had made cookies for Santa, left a carrot out for Rudolph, and tucked our two children in bed just after reading a short version of the Christmas story. All was prepared for Christmas morning.

But now with her eyes peering into mine I realized that she had gotten out of bed before we had prepared the camera so that we could capture the scene of her finding a half eaten cookie, a slightly chewed carrot, and an empty glass of milk.

Our two-year old Amanda had already made her way to the Christmas tree and discovered the "evidence." Her eyes were full of questions but then came the words, "Daddy, where is baby Jesus?"

Okay, I am a minister who is supposed to come up with religious sounding answers. "Where is baby Jesus?" I mean I could show her the cookie crumbs, the nibbled carrot, the presents left by Santa, but she wanted to see the baby. Then it dawned on me that this child of innocence not yet squandered must have listened as her father announced the night before that this was "the evening of our dear savior's birth." So, where is the baby?

With her eyes still looking into mine and before I could come up with some wise words, she asked another question, "He is up at the church?"

He obviously was not "under the tree" and she did not seem to care about the tale-tale signs of a jolly old elf and his reindeer that were spread all around. She wanted to know where baby Jesus was?

Perhaps I spend my living and my life trying to answer Amanda's questions. All of us who seek to follow the child of Bethlehem are seeking to live into Amanda's questions.

And a little child shall lead them . . .

Years later another child offered another "lead." I was pretending to be the innkeeper on one of those years when Christmas came on Sunday. I told my people that if they would show up and not allow Santa to totally capture the morning that I would feed them doughnuts and coffee. I then promised them that there would not be a sermon but I would tell a story. I urged the parents to bring their children so that we could remember "the real meaning of Christmas."

Having been bribed with doughnuts and the promise of "no sermon" a lot of parents and children did show up. I was "into" the innkeeper's story. I got to the part where I was telling about how this rather shabby looking couple showed up late at night after my inn was completely full. I had already recounted how all kinds of people kept making up all kinds of stories and even telling me lies in order to convince me to find room for them in my overcrowded inn.

I went on, "I had quit answering the door but after a rather long period of no one coming to the door I did respond to a knock very late that evening. I thought I had heard all there was to hear but do you know what this man of this shabby couple said to me? 'Please sir do you have a room, my wife is about to have a baby?' I mean does he expect me to believe that?"

In the pregnant pause that followed four-year old Teddy Gellar was standing on the pew beside his mother. Hearing the innkeeper's question Teddy shouted loud enough for everyone to hear, "Yes."

There was an uncomfortable silence at first that filled the sanctuary. You know that kind of silence when someone has said something in church and no one quite knows what to do. Then there came a solitary laugh. Then the place exploded in wonderful laughter, as an innkeeper stood there speechless in front of the crowd.

Teddy had stolen the show and told the story. Into a world of so much "no" Teddy shouted, "yes." It was God's "yes" to all the world's "no."

O, the innkeeper "recovered" and finished the story but he did not really need to. Teddy, a child, told the story in one word. Should the world expect to believe such a story; a story of God being born in a barn after hearing the Innkeepers "no"?

Yes. A little child shall lead them.

20

Mother Mary's Thoughts

O little one, my pain still holds me
but you hold me more
It is your gaze that captures me
on this still night
What must you think as animals
begin their evening rest
beside your manger

You know not of that angel's voice
who told me of your coming
Or do you know more than I imagine
as those eyes of yours meet mine
Your father sleeps, for angel dreams
have tired his weary frame
yet awake he did not believe

Tonight my new love for you shall
be your woven blanket
This world you came to save cannot
have you yet, for you are mine
Soon I will give you up to that other
father who claims you, but
tonight you are simply
my Jesus

21

Poem for Christmas

God, weary of the noise of
pleas unheard
Decided to deafen the world
with a night of silence.

Mary, weary of a journey
too long
Whispered, "let it be so"
and birthed the stable child.

Shepherds, weary of tending
sheep who would be lost
Knelt before a manger because
angel dust filled their eyes.

Now you, weary of traffic and
lists and expectations
Must work to listen and hear again
a night of silence.

22

Swaddling Clothes

THE NEWER TRANSLATIONS SAY, "and they wrapped him in bands of cloth" rather than what I grew up on which is, "and she brought forth her first born child and wrapped him in swaddling clothes and laid him in a manger." For the most part I like the newer translations but sometimes you can throw the baby out with the bath water. And in this case the baby is wrapped in swaddling clothes.

There are just a few old phrases that are like a pair of favorite old pants. Sure the new style pants are "in" but don't you dare throw away my favorite old pants. They may not be in style but they fit in all the right places. They are like old friends.

"Swaddling clothes" is my "favorite pants" kind of phrase. It sounds right. Bands of cloth are something you wrap an old piece of sewing material in but not a baby. I know I am about to get wrapped with the "fact" that "in fact" swaddling clothes means "bands of cloth." So the translators are right but that does not make them "good."

The fact is that back in Mary and Joseph's day new parents did "in fact" wrap infants in tight bands of cloth to make sure that their legs and arms grew straight. This binding was done for up to "six months." You mean to tell me that Jesus started out in a straight jacket even though later his worried mother would call him "crazy"?

This is a dead giveaway that Jesus is really human. After all who does the binding? It is his mother Mary. Joseph and Mary wash the new born baby off and then rub him down with a good "rubbing" of salt to prevent infection. Then on with the "straight jacket" of swaddling clothes to assure that baby Jesus' arms will be firm and to assure that he will not be bow-legged.

This is a detail that bares paying attention to. Why do all of this? After all this is "baby Jesus." This is the famous story of a virgin birth, angels all around, and silent nights. Why perform all of this precautionary stuff to prevent infection and why bind him to make sure his arms and legs end up straight?

"Swaddling clothes" may be the most important phrase in the entire bible. It means that Jesus was and is "one of us." The Hebrew word for "to swaddle" is the same word used to describe the binding up of a broken bone. Are things coming into focus?

Jesus is not the unfeeling, plastic figurine in the nativity scenes we collect. In one of my favorite "manger sets" the tiny arms and legs of a quite naked baby Jesus are reaching upward as if he is waiting for some-one to pick him up. I like it, I really do, but it is all wrong. There are no swaddling clothes. Seems we have stripped baby Jesus of the real thing.

The "real" Jesus is wrapped up tight to assure that his legs and arms will grow straight. The "real" Jesus is covered with salt, like pickles are covered with a salty solution to "keep them." Jesus is rubbed down with salt to preserve his health because a young Mary thinks that is what a good mother is supposed to do.

The real Jesus is, well, real. He is wrapped up with bindings for all of our brokenness. He is "bound" in order to set us free. He is hemmed in that we might grow. His legs and arms need to be straight because some-day, all too soon, they will be stretched out on a tree.

And it all starts with "swaddling clothes." This is a vital indicator as to how real God is going to get. Jesus does not drop out of the sky. He is "brought forth" from Mary and wrapped up tight for us. Mary wants her son's legs and arms straight and she wants them to be strong. The angel announces a divine birth but a very human mother who will know real labor pains wants her son to be "wrapped" and real.

I'm not sure what your "favorite" manger scene depicts. Most of the ones I've seen show a rather angelic type child with a rather lose array of something like "cloth" hanging around his "Gerber" shaped body. Now do not go and sell your nativity sets at the next garage sale because they are not "authentic." That is not the point.

Manger scenes, after all, are not real. They are made of wood or ce-ramics, or plastic. They are fine for what they are.

Just remember that the real Jesus was wrapped in swaddling clothes. Yea, somebody had to cut the cord, clean him up, and wrap the Christmas package. Thanks be to God. The next time you are "broken" by the crooked ways of life remember a child whose mother wrapped him tight so that he would grow up straight.

"Swaddling clothes . . ." the most important words in the bible.

23

Time for Christmas

It was Mary's time for
she was full of life
and questions.
It was Joseph's time for
he wondered how he
would respond to "daddy."

It was an innkeeper's time
as he anticipated extra revenue
and full rooms.
It was shepherd's time
because all they had was time
and lonely nights.

It was stargazer's time as
they searched for meaning
in a night sky.
It was Herod's time and
he dared not share it
with any upstart king.

It was God's time to
create a story to be told
time and time again.
And now it is our time to
silence the ticking clock
and listen to angel voices.

24

To Listen

Mary had to listen
not so much to the
pounding of her young heart
but to the breeze
that carried
an angel's voice

Joseph had to listen
not to the anger
that swelled up in his doubting
mind but to a thunderous dream
that promised a child not his
but ours

Shepherds had to listen
to what seemed like
dancing fire that escaped
into their evening watch
telling them to kneel
in a nearby stable

Now you and I have to listen
to overhear the story
of an unmarried mother
a questioning father
wandering shepherds
and to a God who
wonders if we will listen

25

Epiphany: Sunshine on a Cloudy Day

My GENERATION GREW UP on the beach music sound of, "My Girl." The song begins with a line that brings people to the dance floor to do the shag, "I've got sunshine on a cloudy day, and when it's cold outside, I've got the month of May." What can make the singer of the song "feel this way?" Why, it's "my girl" of course.

Epiphany is the season of sunshine on cloudy days. After the bright star-shine of Christmas the spiritual pilgrim discovers that the clouds do not all flee away. The Christmas tree is on the curb and strings of lights are returned to the attic. The "son" has been "delivered" but there are a mixture of clouds and "sunshine" in the forecast.

One of the misunderstandings prevalent in church going circles is that if one is "saved" or in the proper relationship with God the darkness is banished. Carl Jung, using the principals of depth psychology, conveys that the idea is not to focus on points of light but to make the darkness conscious.

Epiphany is a reminder that the light shines in the darkness and the darkness does not overcome it. The darkness is still around and sometimes very deep.

The stories that begin the season of Epiphany are vivid reminders of the light and the darkness. Wise men go home a different direction figuring that the King whom they first consult in order to discover the whereabouts of the hoped for star child, is up to no good. If they hang around they witness the "slaughter of the innocents."

A starry, starry night quickly ushers in a dark night of the soul for a large number of mothers in Bethlehem who witness genocide only because they happen to live in the same village where a manger is filled with a long awaited promise. Try telling those mothers that the light has finally come to a dark world. All they know is that their young male children are put to the sword because King Herod is filled with jealousy and fear.

The early church evidently used the season of Epiphany to commemorate not only the wise men's visit but also Jesus' baptism and his first miracle at Cana. His birth may have been thrown in for good measure since Christmas has not yet been invented.

The light does not last too long at Jesus' baptism either. As soon as the sun breaks through the clouds a loud clap of thunder is heard which to some sounds like, "Hey this is my boy, am I proud of him. Listen up." But before the press gathers round and the spotlights of cameras frame the new star, Jesus is off into the wilderness to do battle with none other than the Prince of Darkness Grim. Can't the guy at least enjoy his new-found notoriety for a brief moment? Evidently not.

The miracle at Cana is perhaps the only real "full of light" event. O, there is darkness all right. Most families in Jesus' time do not really have the money to have a wedding feast but they do it anyway just to show the Romans that the Chosen People might seem to be captive but no one can capture their spirits.

So in the midst of the darkness the people dance and party because this new married couple means that the "nation" will go on no matter what. The only dark moment comes when the wine runs out. With everyone sobering up too soon the reality of their oppression will become apparent in the midst of the party, so Jesus conveniently makes some more wine for the crowd. Jesus becomes the Lord of the Dance and the life of the party.

I used this image the Sunday after that first September 11. It seems that in spite of towers falling and fears consuming the land we had scheduled "Music Sunday" with liturgical dancers and all. At first I thought we should cancel the dancing. I mean how could we dance in the shadow of September 11?

Then I thought of Cana and the way the people of God thumbed their noses at the hated enemy and partied in spite of their condition. The Romans must have wondered, "How can these people dance in the face of their bleak situation?"

The Romans are not familiar with one of the theme songs of the Jewish people. It sounds something like, "My Girl," and when they hear the first lines all the Jewish folks take to the dance floor. The song begins with "How shall we sing the Lord's Song in a strange land?" The people learned that the way you do so is to put on your dancing shoes and shag in the face of the enemy.

How do you sing the Lord's Song in a strange land? You simply sing it even when it's dark outside.

John Wesley, the founder of the Methodist Movement supposedly said to a young preacher who was struggling with his own faith, "Preach faith until you have faith." So the people dance until there is a reason to dance or they die trying.

Epiphany means manifestation. What is manifest in Epiphany is that the light is in the darkness and the darkness, though very dark, cannot overcome it. So, put on your dancing shoes, light a candle in the darkness, strike up the "I've Been Born Again, Again" tune, and celebrate your baptism because it's Epiphany.

26

Light in the Darkness

IT WAS A TIME of deep darkness. It was a time when hope seemed like a forgotten word. It was a time of despair.

Sounds like that time when the Magi showed up does it not? But I am not referring to that first visit of the Wise Men. I am remembering Jeff and Kelly Watson on the eve of another Epiphany season a number of years ago.

Jeff was a young soon to be father. He had discovered the cancer just after the news of Kelly's pregnancy. The joy of their first child was overshadowed by the battle with cancer.

It was a tough battle. Jeff fought hard. Kelly tried to be brave. Anna was born. Anna was a thin point of light in the ensuing darkness, but Jeff was loosing the battle.

As I prepared to go the hospital on Monday morning I knew I had to compose a newsletter article by the noon deadline. I also had to turn in a sermon title for the next Sunday, which would be the first Sunday of Epiphany. I was not very inspired. I was between leftover Christmas and the coming death of a young father.

I wrote a poem about light in the darkness. I used the image of headlights shining around the dark corner. When it came time for a sermon title I settled on that same theme, "Headlights Around a Dark Corner," would be the title.

As I rose from the computer to go the hospital I wondered to myself, "What is all this headlight stuff?" I dropped the article and the sermon title by the office and headed to the hospital. I knew the inevitable had to be soon.

Kelly was tired. She leaned into my arms and said, "Why can't I at least have a sign that Jeff is going to be okay. Why can't he tell me he sees something or hears something? You know how others say they see a figure of light or a relative who had died and who is waiting for them. Can't I have something?"

I held her and wished that Jeff had said something to me in my time spent with him as he suffered with his illness. I had nothing to give Kelly that morning except the assurance that God was in the midst of this dark time . . . somewhere.

As I turned to leave, she grabbed my hand and said; "He did say something strange early this morning that did not make any sense. Jeff rose up out of the bed and pointed toward the wall and said, 'What are those headlights?' Of course I did not see any headlights. Do you think that meant something?"

My knees almost buckled. "What did you say," I asked? "He said he saw headlights." I put my arms on Kelly's shoulders and told her to lean against the wall because I had something to give her that she would not believe. I told her about my poem and the sermon title. I told her I had no idea why the image came to me.

I held her as we both cried a bit. The light shines in the darkness and the darkness cannot overcome it.

This is Epiphany. Kelly remarried and lives in another city. I saw Anna a few years later at a restaurant with her grandparents. She was visiting for Christmas. Her smile is beautiful. And Jeff, well, Jeff is driving the car with those headlights.

Epiphany is the season of the light that shines in the darkness.

27

Distant Star

A Poem for Epiphany

Distant star of someone else's longing
shine into our waiting darkness
Your light led seekers whose dreams
wanted reality's waking knowledge.

Are you there in our night sky or
does the horizon of our doubt hide you?
Looking down, we need some headlights
to give hope around our dark curves.

Could it be that any star could point
the way to the light of long ago?
For now all the stars shine on our place
of revelation if we but have eyes to see.

We are all stardust filled with light from
a hand that scattered worlds.
O to look and see the light that shines....
this ... this is the chance for Epiphany.

28

Standing in Line

Jesus' Baptism: Matthew 3:13–17

Who are you stranger
      standing there awaiting
  cool waters that contain
      refining fire
      for our stale
         old
         sins?

You say nothing—you seem
      lost as you look
  toward some far horizon
      into some unknown
      future where
         fate
         seals lives

Step up—come out of your
      solitary trance and
  see that it is your turn
      for John to
      make you new
         in
         Jordan's waters

Now it is the baptizer
who seems lost
frozen in front of
your waiting face
but you bow below
waters
that bury you

And then the thunder surrounds
the others who wait
with you—standing in line
and some divine voice
rains down
wet words—
"He's the one—
my wet
wonderful
son"

29

Lent: The Necessary Wilderness

THE BIBLE IS FULL of wilderness but in our fast paced, avoid pain at all cost, kind of culture we manage to create various bypasses around the wilderness. My grandmother used to say, "What's with all this happiness stuff?"

At 93 she reflected about necessary pain that comes with life fully lived. Happiness is something that happened in between the necessary pain. These days we feel that we are "entitled" to happiness. The Constitution gives us permission to "pursue happiness" so we set our emotional cruise controls and go for it.

The season of Lent is about the need for wilderness. Somehow God feels that the human spirit needs time to do without. This is even truer in an environment of over stimulation. What is interesting is that in an effort to avoid the "void" of the wilderness we seem to create a kind of hectic wilderness and do not even know it is wilderness. It does not "feel" like the wilderness because there is so much going on. But if we were to be pulled out of the snapshot and allowed to see all that is piled on top of us we might discover that we are in a wilderness of "too much."

As the poet once wrote, "the center cannot hold," and we become compartmentalized. Life as an integrated whole is lost to speed.

The real wilderness is a place where we simplify because we have to. In Jesus' wilderness the people knew they needed to conserve water so they paid attention to how much they were drinking. The barren places allow one to see the wonder of the ordinary.

Jesus immediately goes into the wilderness as a first act after his baptism. He needs time to reflect and ponder. He fasts in order to gain perspective about priorities.

Out there in the stark reality of the wilderness Jesus comes face to face with not only his demons but also "the" demon. The powers of darkness always seem to know our names because they abide within us. We do not have to believe in some devil to realize the power of the dark side.

An old expression is that the devil is in the details, but today perhaps a better truth is that he devil is in the distractions. We are a distracted people. I recently listened to the "details" of a study about what people do while driving a car. Talking on cell phones used to be the biggest distraction but now there are iPods, CD multiple changers, GPS screens, even video monitors that can be installed in the front seat so that he driver will not miss the latest installment of a favorite show.

Jesus goes immediately into the wilderness each year on the first Sunday of the Lenten season. There are few distractions in the wilderness. What is the lesson here for the human spirit? There is a time for doing without rather than always getting more.

In his book, "How to Want What You Have," Timothy Miller discovers that evolution has bred the human being to "crave." Craving has become a natural tendency and therefore must be resisted or it will take over. Wanting what we do not have is "instinctual," according to this book.[1]

The premise of the book you are now reading is that if this is true then the human spirit is diminished and not built up by this craving. Jesus goes into the place of fasting and scarcity to discover who he really is. Sure "the devil" tempts him with the "more" of life: more food, more excitement, and more power. But remember that the old story says this more is bad for both Jesus and us.

In "How to Want What You Have," Miller suggests that there are three principals that can help with this instinct toward craving what we do not have. He writes that the word "enough" is not in our instinctual dictionary.[2] The wilderness may be necessary to rediscover what is below our instinctual drives for more.

The three principals are attention, compassion, and gratitude. I would suggest that Jesus knows this before this book is written. One can truly pay attention in the wilderness because you are away from distractions. Compassion is gained due to the simplicity of the wilderness. We are given the chance to realize the interdependence of all life from lizards

---

1. Miller, *How to Want What You Have*, 76.

2. Ibid., 16–17.

to the life cycle of a cactus. And gratitude is manifests because in the midst of doing without one can really be grateful for what one has.

The noise of the I Pod and the constant stimulation of cell phones ringing make us less attentive, less compassionate, and lacking in gratitude. Lent gives the pilgrim in a strange land the chance to stop and do without for a while.

30

Ash Wednesday: Branded with a Cross

Each Ash Wednesday I participate in a conspiracy of sorts. I always ask my music folks to make sure we have at least two children's choirs sing for the evening service. I do this for two reasons. The first is that it will get their parents to the service, parents who would have otherwise stayed home and watched "Desperate Housewives" or "American Idol."

The second reason is that I love to put the sign of the cross on the eager, smiling heads of the children who are there because they were asked to sing. They love getting "branded" with the cross. I tell them to go home and take a good look at their foreheads before they go to sleep.

"This is God's way of saying 'I love you and you are mine,'" I tell them. The children are used to getting their hands stamped with some emblem to get them back into an amusement park or "Chucky Cheese" so they understand what it means to be "marked." They really like this sign stuff so it gets the parents attention.

When I put the sign of the cross on the children I do not use the solemn words, "Remember you are dust and to dust you shall return. Repent and believe the gospel." Those words are too heavy for children. Heck they may be too heavy for adults.

I say to the children as I "ash" them, "This is a sign of God's love for you."

The adults get the heavy stuff because supposedly we can handle it and we need it. What is it that we need on Ash Wednesday?

In a world where the river of denial runs deep we need to be reminded what we are made of. We are "dust." This is not so popular to espouse. Most commercials tell us we are made of components that need to be "made up" with all kinds of stuff for our faces and hair. We are made of "stuff" that needs to ride around in brightly colored pieces of metal with satellite radios playing our favorite music so that we will not hear the harsh sounds of the traffic and the world.

But Ash Wednesday is about dirt. According to the old story we are but God breathed dirt. It is supposed to be a humbling moment when ashes are put on our forehead. Humility is not so evident these days. We are into the self-esteem thing or the purpose driven thing. No one wants to feel like dirt.

Ash Wednesday, however, is not so much about feeling bad as it is about feeling grateful that the one who breathes life into the dirt really knows and loves us enough to, well, die for the dirt. It is the "who me" moment when the realization that the best thing God ever did hung on a cross for dirty old you.

It is also a time to begin a process of repentance and self-examination, two more things that are not so popular in the "lost while making excellent time" kind of world we occupy. To repent means that we have to slow down long enough to "turn." Jesus would have known the Hebrew word for "repent," which is *tushuva*. *Tushuva* means to turn around and take a good look.

Someone once told me that in Jesus' day there was a point in camel caravans that you stopped and checked the level of water in your water bags. In the desert if you did not have enough water to make it to the next oasis you would die so you better turn around and go back for the nearest water. This point was called the *tushuva* point.

How about a new road sign that would simply read, *Tushuva* Now! That is the sign on the road for Ash Wednesday, along with the dusty sign of the cross. It means, "Slow down you are approaching a Cross road."

31

Dream Dust

A Poem Offered to Prepare for Ash Wednesday

They wanted so to hold
the victory in
their hands
for there had been
so much emptiness—
"Fill us with dreams,"
they shouted.
So they gathered round
him like hungry
children needing bread
for growling were their
souls from malnutrition—
"Blessed are the poor,"
he said.
What is this foolish wisdom
taught by a fisher
of people whose
nets seem quite empty and
whose words seem anemic—
"Blessed are you who weep,"
he whispered.
What is this dream dust we
now hold in our hands
as we wonder—
and with the ashes of
hopes that failed us
we find new life

"Behold I make all things new."
The ashes on our foreheads
are dream dust
to remind us who we are
and bring us home
around his cross
of love.

32

It's Not Supposed to Be Easy

I REMEMBER THOSE DREADED days of summer practice for High School football. Back in the dark ages, football shoes had those heavy cleats. This was before the days of "Air Jordon" type shoes with all sorts of lightweight extras and cushioned support.

The football shoes of "back then" were, well, heavy and plain. But you had to wear them to play football.

Before the soon to be glory days of Friday nights and the screaming crowds under the lights there had to come the August days of practice and what I hated most, leg raises. The coach would bark out the word, "up" and then start counting. A group of would be football stars would lift our legs while lying in the early morning dew laced grass. It seemed that the coach counted in "Southern style," real slow.

My abdominal muscles would start to quiver as the numbers sounded across the humid summer air, "14, 15, 16." Beyond the time when my abs would begin to ache would come the longed for word, "down." Collective groans could be heard as our shoes hit the ground. In the midst of the agony came the word, "up."

It was not supposed to be easy. The coach, while he may have seemed like the kind of guy who received his training from some masochistic outfit, was trying to get young bellies prepared for the impact of football helmets in the gut. Soft bellies needed to become firm and strong. This was practice, after all. The real game was down the road.

Lent is not supposed to be easy. It is a kind of training ground for Christians who have developed "soft places" in our lives. Jesus comes along with that cross of his and offers it to us again. Then comes the dreaded word, "up."

God must know that over the year we have gotten flabby in our discipleship. Lectures given and sermons heard are like so many plays drawn on a blackboard. Such words will not get us in shape. The "play-book" gives some needed instructions, but words on a page will not prepare us for the real "game."

We have to lift up the burdens of broken promises, spiritual detours, and plain old laziness. It can be painful. During the long slow counting of the season we call Lent we may long for someone to shout, "down" before the needed conditioning takes place.

Do not fear. The one who is walking between the rows of groaning disciples is the one who has done his on "ups and downs." He knows the pain. He has felt it. He knows the temptations to take the short cuts.

This one who says to us, "up" does not do so from some distant coaching tower overlooking a field of struggling disciples. He is the one whose nickname is Emmanuel, God with us. If you look beside you, you might just notice that the one down there groaning with you is the same one who earlier shouts out the ups and downs. He may look over your way from down there in the grass and say, "Come on you can do it. Here, I'll do some with you. Now up."

He has groaned our groans. He won his own game in overtime. It was quite an upset. The odds were stacked against him, but he had done his conditioning.

It is not supposed to be easy, but we need it. Now, "up."

33

These Hands

Jesus' Time of Temptation Based on Matthew 4:1–11

THESE HANDS HAVE SHAPED wood. My father taught me well the craft. Now a voice I have heard before wants me to shape bread from stones. I remember how my mother shaped bread with those same hands that stroked my cheek as she sang songs to me late in the evenings. O Mary, sing one of those songs now. It is so lonely and the stones seem to be calling to me.

How wise he is to make me remember my mother's bread. The past seems so much more certain than the future. As I stand on this mountain I can see the distant horizon and I sense that beyond it is a danger that escapes my mother's reach. There is no song for such a time. There is only silence and the wind speaking my name; offering me another song. Such power is tempting. The song has an easy melody.

So far down is the bottom of this rocky spire. I feel as if I could fall. Is it the hunger that makes me light headed or all the songs competing to be heard? I must sit down before he pushes me too far.

This stone I hold in my hand. . . . it does look like bread. You do not like my laughter do you, O Tempter? But that is all you shall hear this day. These hands shall not do your bidding. These hands are for wood, and my songs are not for you.

I shall sleep now and let the angels come as they did after those late night lullabies at Mary's breast. Go away. You and I both know there will be other days.

These hands will make you no bread today. We will both have to rest with our hunger.

34

Some Other Way

A Poem for Lent

Bid me come some other way
    not this narrow path
    where shadows seem to
        bear the shape of crosses.
    I would wish for beams of sunlight
    to brighten footsteps lightened
    from unbridled freedom
        and joy easily gained.

But still you stand there and
    ask if I will go with you
    to a place of giving up
        and letting go.
    Could it be that I need some of
    this death you offer
    instead of the constant
        layered life that covers me?

Timidly I will go with you
    on that journey you
    have traveled before and ask,
        "Where is my cross?"

35

Holy Week: The Cost of Love
Itemized List for the Cost of Holy Week

<u>Item</u>	<u>Cost</u>
Palm Branches—	free (although it cost the Palm trees)
One colt on which Jesus rode—	free (borrowed)
Clothes spread on the road in—	free (someone had to replace)
Possible legal fees—	legal action taken by Money Changers in the Temple against Jesus for assault and disruption of business (cost unknown)
Loss of revenue—	(cost unknown) even Money Changers have to make a living
One "Last Supper"—	supplies of herbs, lamb, bread wine (the cost of what Jesus said the bread and wine were = one life)
Betrayal—	the only exact figure on the list = 30 pieces of silver (although Judas paid dearly for the silver)
Sleeping disciples while Jesus prayed—	a broken heart
Jesus' prayer in the garden—	"sweat like drops of blood"
Peter's denial—	tears, shame
Trial by Pilate—	loss of one night's sleep and a bowl of water for hand washing

Purple robe and crown of thorns—	free (supplied by angry soldiers)
Cross—	free (willingly supplied by the government-but you know how it is with the government- somebody has to pay somewhere, sometime)
Tomb for Jesus burial—	(no money to buy a plot) borrowed grave
One resurrection—	free, but not cheap

Total cost: (unknown)

Amount paid: (mostly unknown, although the amount paid by God is totaled as "one only begotten child")

Payback schedule: (still being decided: suggested form of payment/love offering)

36

Father, Your Shoes Are Hard to Fill

Reflections of Jesus in the Garden of Gethsemane

O Father, your shoes are hard to fill—
   My feet seemed so small
but I have tried to walk
   the path you put
     before me

My shoes were still moist from
   John's shower of blessing
when he whispered to me, "I am
   not worthy to untie your sandal,"
     and I said, "Baptize me, John."

My feet stumbled upon the rugged
   slope of the mountain
that day in the wilderness
   when Satan wanted
     me to try on other shoes

It was tempting, father, but I
   told him the shoes
would not fit, for my feet
   were set toward this
     place of another trial

Sweet was that day the woman knelt
  at my feet and bathed them
with tears of her devotion
  and the perfume of an ointment
    beyond reason

My disciples did not want me to touch
  their feet that night I
knelt and removed their shoes
  and washed them of their
    pride with healing waters

My feet are tired, father, for
  I have walked long
in obedience to your hard way—
  Can I rest them now
    for no disciple washes my feet?

Where must these feet go, father
  in order to find rest?
I see visions of my feet broken
  on a rough wood
    nailed down with hate

Your shoes are hard to fill, father—
  Must it be so painful to
keep in step with a people so
  out of step with you
    and your ways for them?

The souls of my feet ache, Abba
  from years of attempting to stand
in your place with so much
  resting on these shoulders—
    stepping toward this time

I kneel just now, my feet cradled
   beneath the longing body
of one who yearns to know
   if other feet will follow
      in my steps, along the way

Your shoes are hard to fill, father
   but I have tried, like a
child who wants to fill a father's
   shoes and grow up to be
      like, like father, like son

Your shoes are hard to fill—
   but now—for now
not mine, but your will

Time now to rise and walk your way
   so hold my weary feet in
your hands, father
   and wash them in some
      cool waters of a life eternal

37

Hide Me

The Thoughts of Simon Peter after the Denial

Hide me, O earth or swallow
   me sky and lift me away from
     the shame and sorrow.
Judas was consistent with his betrayal
   but I was like the candle flame
     hot but wavering.

Raging in the garden, I was like
   some child making up for sleeping
     when he asked me to watch.
Running with the rest, for fear was
   my only friend on that black night
     of lost causes and dead dreams.

"You are one of his disciples" came words
   taking me from my hiding, but I
     buried my head in denial.
The rooster's call found me out
   and the "rock" crumbled as
     he promised I would.

And now it is the third day that
   he spoke of with mysterious words
     but I have no faith left to hope them true.
He is hidden in his grave and I am
   revealed to be wind and dust, no rock
     for I am lost and he is gone.

But what does this vacant tomb say
  and now they steal even his broken body
    as they have stolen our dreams.
Or, could it be that God has fooled
  not only Simon but Death itself
    hide me, my Lord, in such foolishness.

38

Say Something

Observing Jesus before Pilate and at the Cross

A ruler screams into your
    dark sorrowful eyes,
      "For God's sake, say something."
But you have spoken all
    that is needed:
      —upon a mountain of beatitudes
      —beside a well with a lost woman
      —into the face of a rich man
    who could not let go
      —answering angry religious rulers
    and refusing to hush a crowd
    with words that say,
      "Even the stones
        will cry out."

And so you stand there
    saying almost nothing—
Sad as if the weight of
    the world is on
      your shoulders—
But then, it is . . .

Do you wonder in this
    distant quiet
    that you seem
    to hold so gently
      in your eyes—

Do you wonder if it will
        make a difference?
Will your quiet pose cause
        others to
        speak words of hope
As they remember what you
        do this day of sorrows?

And now you see the basin of water
        and the washing of hands
        to wipe away guilt
And you remember their feet
        you washed the other
        night mid stares
            of disbelief

Maybe you do need to say
        something—for no
        one understands this
        silence
And those you have chosen
        to carry on your kingdom
        are hiding in the shadows
            of denial
            fear, and loss

No . . . you have spoken all there
        is to say
Except for a few utterances
        from your pain
        which cannot be
        contained
            for a cross
            will pull it
            from your
                quiet
            dying spirit

If we listen amidst shouts
        of condemnation and
        the clamor of injustice
You will speak your last—
        "Forgive them—
        I thirst—
        O, mother—
        I am forsaken—
        Today . . . in paradise—
        Receive my spirit—
        It is finished"

Say something—
        even now . . .
No, it is time for
        a silence to
        hear your
            deep love
                for us . . .

39

Eulogy for Jesus / Pieta

HE WAS A FRIEND to many so I do not understand why he is being refused a decent burial. The religious leaders want no part in saying any words over him so it is left to me to offer a brief thought about his life.

He was buried earlier in a barrowed grave. There was not even a graveside service. He was hurriedly wrapped in some grave clothes and laid to rest with no fanfare or liturgy of the dead. This one who offered so many interpretations of religious concepts and rituals had no words said at his grave so I rise now to say a few things about his life.

I am not sure about his age though he seemed young. I asked about his place of birth and was surprised to hear that he was supposedly born in a place where animals were kept for the night. His hometown seems to have been Nazareth where there still are stories told about the strange circumstances of his birth.

It seems that his father Joseph saved his mother Mary from shame by marrying her even though the rumor was that the child she was carrying was not his. Jesus' father preceded him in death but again I am not sure when this happened.

He seemed to mention his mother on occasion but reference to his father became part of his theological teaching. Part of the reason for his untimely death seems to be that he kept talking about a heavenly father. To talk about God as "father" is one thing and quite acceptable, but to talk of God as one's father as if you are the only Son of God is not acceptable.

The quick trial that was held to accuse Jesus of blasphemy brought all of this out in the open. As you can see none of his tiny band of disciples are here to offer any words of defense about these accusations so all I can say is what I have heard.

The reality that none of them are here speaks loudly of his final few days. It seems his disciples were quite present and noticeable at the parade held in his honor a few days ago but they are nowhere to be found now. I was told that one of the Jewish leaders named Nicodemus helped with the burial of Jesus since none of his disciples came to pay their last respects.

Part of the reality is that they all seem to be afraid for their own lives. The leader of the disciples known as Simon sometimes called "the rock" was overheard vehemently denying that he had ever known Jesus. Another of his disciples, Judas, actually sold him out for a few pieces of silver. Judas led the authorities to a secret place and identified Jesus as the one to be taken. He actually did this with a kiss and embrace.

I am not sure what Jesus did to deserve such treatment by those closest to him but all I can say is a few good things about the man. I think he deserves at least that because it seems that with such loyalty by those who were supposed to spread what he called the gospel these words may be all that is remembered about the man.

After the troubling rumors surrounding his birth Jesus seems to have lived a fairly normal life in and around his hometown of Nazareth. He had a strange episode when he was 12 years old when his parents brought him here to Jerusalem for a festival and he seems to have baffled the scribes and elders with his knowledge of the scriptures.

John baptized Jesus, son of Joseph, in the zealous movement that John had before Herod beheaded him. Jesus stood in line with all the rest for his baptism but some said that when he came up out of the water a thunderous sound echoed over the valley.

Jesus then disappeared for a number of days. He told those standing by that day that he had to go into the wilderness to discover what kind of leader God needed him to be.

I do not know what happened in that wilderness but I can tell you that he came out of it to select an interesting assortment of folks to be his inner band of disciples. Among them were some fishermen, a member of the fanatic zealot group who wanted to overthrow Rome, and a tax collector. Considering what has happened over the past few days he obviously should have chosen better.

Jesus became rather famous for his miracles. I really do not understand why the religious leaders did not consider some of these as evidence of his claim to be the long awaited Christ.

Supposedly he even brought people back to life from the dead. I mean what more do people want from a Messiah?

He was kind but he was tough. He even told his own mother one time that he now had other parents. Those who listened to God were his parents.

Yet his kindness was apparent not only in whom he had around him but also in his many stories. He loved children even though our customs deny children any say so or rights. He had women in his following even though the religious teachers think this is too much too soon. Some of those women had some terrible reputations but that seemed not to matter to him. In fact the more trouble they were in the more he seemed attracted to them.

Not only did one of his stories include having a Samaritan as the hero of the story Jesus also seems to have befriended a Samaritan woman one afternoon. They're still telling that story.

Even though he will soon be lost to history I will tell you that he loved the lost of life. His favorite images seem to be around lost things: lost coins, lost sheep, even lost children.

The way of life he offered is both extreme and somewhat bizarre. He spoke of loving enemies, turning cheeks, and walking extra miles. I admire him for such a different way of looking at life but it seems our world is not ready for such teachings.

I feel compassion for his mother and one of his closest followers another Mary from Magdala. Along with some other women they watched as he was crucified. They had to listen as he spoke his last words from a dreaded Roman cross.

I offer you these words of testimony about Jesus today because first of all none of his supposed friends are to be found and second because I too watched him die and stood at a distance to see them bury him. Jesus spoke words of forgiveness for those who hammered the spikes into his already beaten body. He muttered some words of compassion for his watching mother. No matter what anybody says about this man he at least died as he lived, with forgiveness on his lips.

My heart this day goes out to him and I feel I must offer these words of testimony because of one of the last things he said. He forced his head up to the dark sky. His face was streaked with dried blood from the crown of thorns they had forced onto his head. He paused for a moment and then screamed, "My God, my God, why have you forsaken me?"

Then he whispered something else but I could not make it out. There really was not anything else to be said. Words were empty after that. He died a few moments later.

I offer this brief testimony to the man whom some thought to be the Christ. His selection of friends and followers might be called into question but his deep love for people should be remembered this day of his death. He longed to offer a new way of life to this world but this world is not ready for his kind of life. It seems we are only ready for his death.

I was close by when they took him from the cross. His mother held him one last time. I suppose it was prying but I got as close as I could. I later wrote down what I remembered her saying. I leave you with her words about him:

PIETA

Mary Holding the Body of Jesus after the Crucifixion

Playing as a child—that
    day you fell against
    the rocks on the
        hillside of Nazareth
I held you as you wept
    and watched the red
        of life seep from
            your wound

Now I hold you—fallen
    again upon the rough
    landscape of a world
        not yet ready for you
O my son, how empty of life
    you now are because
        you were too full of
            your father's love

Some angel's voice—now
    so distant on this
    tortured hill of death

told me of your coming
Pounding like nails in my
hearing is only your cry
of dying so alone
for heaven must be empty

Look what they have done—your
body so torn from the
hate you came to quiet
and now that quiets you
Some stranger offers you his
own tomb of death
for I have nothing to
give you but my tears

40

Easter: Empty Promises

THE SEASON OF EASTER begins with empty promises. Women go to a
tomb carrying spices and broken promises. They come up empty or
at least they come upon an empty tomb.

Ever since this quite remarkable and unbelievable story is told people
have been trying to fill that empty tomb. Pilate and his cronies spread the
word that the tomb is not empty at all but is full of lies. The "truth" is that
the disciples have pulled a fast one and have stolen the body and put it
somewhere for safekeeping.

Ciaphas and the rest of the crowd who have pulled off a trial that has
all the makings of a lynching party are sure that the only thing empty on
that "third day" is the empty bag where 30 pieces of silver are "emptied" in
front of them by a disappointed Judas. Resurrection is not real no matter
what kind of fanciful tales grief stricken women and cowardly disciples
want to dream up. These rumors are simply more empty promises made
by the followers of yet another Messiah; rumors that the "real church" has
to rid itself of in order to protect the people and keep the peace.

As I write this the empty tomb is filled with another book proclaiming that the tomb is in fact quite full, at least the tomb called the "Jesus
tomb" is occupied. Why there is even DNA evidence to prove that long
ago promises of resurrection are and were quite empty.

Easter begins with empty promises. Somehow we are to believe that
the original tomb that holds a crucified Messiah is "in fact" empty. I do not
know how God pulls this off. The body of Jesus is not simply a resusci-
tated corpse because it passes through doors and seems to transport itself
from one scene to another in an instant.

Quantum physics and Einstein's theory of relativity has not yet been
"invented" but it seems that God is impatient. Matter, it seems can change
and even time can change at the speed of light. The old physics that states

83

that one object cannot occupy two places at the same time is turned up-side down.

God does "something" with the body of Jesus of Nazareth. It is a once in a lifetime kind of thing. Our resurrection will not and is supposed to not be like his. God does this for Jesus to show us something and to show the world something. The world has a hard time believing it because it does not fit any analogy that we seem to come up with.

Our promised resurrection is not going to be like this first "empty promise." Our bodies will be "put to rest" either by burial, cremation, or perhaps by giving them to medical research. That which we carry around with us for lo these many years will not "reappear," as does the body of Jesus. We are not "coming back," but Jesus does come back in a once in all eternity kind of event, which really cannot be compared to anything else. Trying to compare his resurrection with something else ends up at a dead end.

This is the reason that no one including those first disciples "understand" what happens in and at the resurrection of Jesus. Those who know Jesus so well do not at first recognize him but through the resurrection appearances he "becomes known to them."

Jesus' tomb is empty but the promises he makes in his appearances are not empty promises. He basically says:

> Now pay attention. My father is not going to do this kind of thing again. I have come back to tell you that there is a place waiting for you so do not be afraid. You are not going to come back like this but I will come for you from that place where I just went. Trust me on this. Now, you have work to do so get to it. There are disciples to be made, baptisms to be done, and feeding of sheep to be handled. What you see and "touch" will not be here in a few days, but what you experience as my presence will be with you always. After your work is done I will be there at your last breath and give you your kind of resurrection. It's a promise.

Easter begins with a kind of "empty promise" that although our "tombs" will be quite full when we die, because of an empty grave long ago we will live again. Those two disciples on the road to Emmaus do not understand this so Jesus has to explain it both by his words and his presence with them. We are on that road again if we seek to follow the Christ of the empty tomb.

Those two disciples are evidently doing the same thing we often do. They are, you guessed it, making excellent time, but they are "lost" in their grief. As Jesus starts speaking to them he offers one of the best and perhaps most humorous lines in the New Testament. Cleopas is talking with "the other disciple" about "all of the things that have happened in the past week." Jesus overhears the two recounting the denials, betrayals, and crucifixion stuff and he asks, "Hey what are you guys talking about?"

Since they are evidently walking too fast to notice who it is who asks the question Cleopas responds, "We are talking about all the things that have happened in recent days." Here comes the line that if we are walking too fast through the story we miss. Jesus asks, "Oh, what things?"

Here is the "reason for the season" speaking to them "in the flesh" and they miss it and him. Jesus must smile as he says, "Oh really, has anything important happened lately. I've been rather busy."

These two "followers" are so preoccupied with the past that they miss the present. One of them responds:

> Are you the only person who has not read the paper or watched the news in the past few days? Have you been in some cave or something? We're talking about our leader and how we hoped he would be the one to deliver this crazy world of ours out of the mess we are in. But now it looks like it was all empty promises.

Jesus then pulls out his pocket Gideon bible and refreshes their faded memories about the promises that are made in the scriptures. He does the research and shows them that the religious pundits of the day including those closest to "this man who is supposed to be the deliverer" have missed some very important old promises contained in the scriptures.

It seems that everyone is in such a hurry to be top dog again and win that no one bothers to see those seemingly obscure passages that say stuff like, "He will be wounded for our transgressions, and with his stripes we will be healed." Everyone who wants to be first in the new "kingdom" has somehow missed those old promises that project a king "who will be a shepherd but who will be led to the slaughter as a ransom for many." Yea, they miss all of this for sure and now they are running so fast to somewhere to get away from all the pain that they are missing it again.

Jesus slows them down and actually brings them to a standstill with his delving into the very scriptures they think they know so well. "Hey, you want something to eat," they ask him? They must want to hear some more about this "new translation" of the ancient text.

"Sure," Jesus says, "Seems like I haven't eaten for days. What ya got?" "Well, we're not sure but I know we can find some bread and uh maybe some wine. Come on just stay a while." "Well, okay, I've got a few more visits I need to make but there's always time for bread and wine," the stranger replies.

The rest is history or at least it is history for those who believe in "empty promises."

Easter is the season when the would be follower of the crucified one realizes that he or she is the unnamed disciple in the road to Emmaus story. Cleopas is named. Why does Luke not name the "other disciple"? It is you. It is me. We are on the road with Jesus making "excellent time" but as usual needing to be "found" by the one whose job it is to find the lost.

41

So Empty

Mary Magdalene at the Tomb

So empty is my heart,
like this borrowed
grave
You were once surrounded in
the darkness of
another Mary's body
Only to give you birth that
they might bury you in
this place
of death

Now they have taken you
from us again
O Lord
Your broken body could not
be left alone
these few days
Even to rest in this rock of
pain and remorse
so empty—
is this place

But then you said you would
not be here
even for me
O, Lord, I have come to wrap you
again in love

and spices of peace
But you are not here and my
hurting faith can not
yet believe
in resurrection

Your cross is empty, your grave
is empty, my heart
is empty
Fill me Lord, with the hope that
your words are true
and death is empty—
O one who tends this garden tell me
where lies his
broken life . . . My Lord, it is you . . . it is you

42

A Stranger on the Road

Based on the Emmaus Road Story in Luke 24

Good news, buried like some headline
that could not make the front page.
Over, like the last page of a book
whose ending was not happy.

To them he might as well have
been dead and buried,
For the third day meant nothing but
three days from when hope died.

Rumors of his rising were just that—
idle tales told by wishful thinkers.
So it was that they were blind to his presence
and deaf to his announcement.

Only when they sat awhile and asked him
to break open reality,
did they see it was Jesus after all . . .
Alive, smiling, and telling them to go
back to where the cross had been.

43

Telling Resurrection

Based on John 20:10–18

It was but days ago that I touched
   tired feet
    bathing his soles
      in costly perfume
wiping his ankles
     with my hair

Those men he chose
   understood not
   what I was doing
     with my touch
for my tears were
      mixed with the fragrance

Then his broken body
   looked down at me
    from that forsaken cross
      and his pierced feet
I longed to touch
     but could not

Now I weep again
   in the garden of death
   because he tells me to
to touch him not
but to go tell a sleeping
      world that he is alive

My tears of flowing joy
   I wipe with these hands
   that bathed his feet
      with promised death
for I shall offer my
      telling touch of resurrection

44

Pentecost: A Really Good Ghost Story

Those first disciples of Jesus are in between a rock and a hard place after the resurrection. The "rock" is Simon Peter and the hard place is the firm reality that all of them know that the rock has crumbled into pieces just a few hours after "the rock" proclaims that, "All other ground is sinking sand but I will be your sure foundation."

"Upon this rock I will build my church," Jesus announces, but shortly thereafter Peter says, "Houston, we have a problem." Peter does not want to be the building block if the "site plan" calls for risk and possible failure. If this rock is supposed to be the foundation for future building someone better "re-survey" the landscape and figure out just what kind of church can be built upon such shifting ground.

Before the events of what we now know as "Passion Week" the disciples are bent on making "excellent time." James and John are ready to be the lead drivers in this race with the rest of the disciples being offered the chance to "draft" their lead cars. Jesus has to pull James and John out of the driver's seats into which they have buckled themselves and jerk a knot in their cords.

"You two have no idea what is ahead at the checkered flag, do you?" asks Jesus. James and John only ask to be number one and number two in the coming Kingdom. They are so intent on getting to the finish line quick that they have not bothered to ask just where they are going. This particular "race" has one final hill at the finish line that James and John do not anticipate. Just over the hill next to the waving checkered flag is a cross. What?

So let's add this up. We have, after the resurrection, a shattered "rock," two would be lead drivers who have no idea what finishing the race means, a sneaky look alike disciple who kisses Jesus and screams "It's him, it's him," a questioning skeptic who insists on sticking his fingers into some fresh wounds before he will buy into believing anything, and a guy named Phillip who on at least one occasion asks; "Uh, well what is the way, or where is the way, or which way is the way?" I'm not even going to mention the many instances in which Jesus looks into the disciple's eyes after he tells one of his stories and says, "You guys just don't get it do you?"

So, before the disciples are sent off into the world to "work the plan" that ends up being "the church of Jesus Christ," the one who starts the movement says to them:

> Listen up. After I'm gone do not hit the road too quick. I'm going to send you something that you will need. And trust me, with your track record you need it. I'm going to send you the Holy Spirit, but you will have to wait on it. You need some time to ponder what all this means and then I will send you, well, don't try to understand this, just trust me this time. This Spirit will be your friend, your guide, and your counsel. You are going to need all three to do what I need you to do.

The miracle is that this time the disciples seem to listen. The story in Acts has them "waiting" in an "upper room." What happens next is a good ghost story. The Holy Spirit used to be called the Holy Ghost, for good reason. The story of dancing tongues of fire and disciples speaking perfect Egyptian with a slight southern Galilean accent is the stuff of good ghost stories.

Those religious tourists who are in Jerusalem for the holiday cannot believe their ears when they hear these local "red necks" speaking in various languages. The analogy would be one of the tourists saying, "Hey I'm from Paris and that guy over there is speaking perfect French, well, with a southern accent, but it is still the King's tongue. How is he doing that? Isn't he from 'around here?'"

It is "spooky" for sure but it is a much-needed story. Pentecost is still needed although many would be disciples treat Pentecost like it is indeed a "ghost story." Tongues of fire and what seems like out of control religious fanatics who speak in "other tongues" are not the fare for pew sitting, hymn singing, stand up sit down, kind of Christians. O, a few "Pentecostals" may get into this but then that's for them not "us."

The truth is that if we are going to slow down and not get "lost while making excellent time," we need Pentecost. Pentecost is a reminder that one who desires to follow Jesus is called not to be a religious tourist but a spiritual pilgrim. James and John are into the express tour business but Jesus changes their plans.

Pentecost means that we who will follow Jesus need some help. This journey of faith is not a self-guided tour but a spirit lead pilgrimage. Disciples of Jesus must "wait" and need to be equipped. The "fast lane" will get you there quicker but with Jesus it is not the getting there that is important. The journey is what is important.

"Are we there yet?" may be the child's anxious question on a trip but for the spiritual pilgrim the response is "Be here now."

Interestingly the season of Pentecost begins the longest season of the Christian year. One must "wait it out" all the way until Advent. This season of pondering and being open to the equipping of the Spirit that comes after Pentecost Day is called "ordinary time." What begins with the extra-ordinary event of tongues of fire suddenly becomes the stuff of the ordinary. So it seems because it is time to get back to business.

"Ordinary" actually means, "to count" from the Latin "ordinal." This is the season that "counts." Why is that? It is the same with the modern day pilgrim as it is with those first disciples. The resurrection has happened so what now?

Are we going to "count for something" or is this whole thing simply a really good ghost story? Is all of this Jesus stuff going to add up to something?

Pentecost is the season that Jesus says to any who will call themselves disciples, "Well, let's see what you are going to do with what I give to you, and by the way slow down and wait. You still need the Spirit."

45

Sun Dried Tomatoes

Based on the Story of Pentecost in Acts 2:1–21

Full of past life they
waited
resembling what they
used to be yet
only in name

Sun dried tomatoes full
of taste
but imprisoned by their
parched sense of
what might be

And then came a wind from
beyond the sun
and life filled their past
and growth that seemed a dream
became more real than ever

Are we like sun dried tomatoes
needing Pentecost—
Stored up life full of
taste but not knowing
the power of life?

Come, fire that parches not
but fills—
Dance over our heads
with tongues of light
and make us alive again

46

Thirsty

Based on John 4, the Story of the Woman at the Well

To fill the jar on my shoulder
　　was my only task
A mindless errand carried out
　　in noon time sun so
as to not disturb nice people
　　who were resting

In his solitude he spoke to me
　　not of empty vessels
But of my parched and thirsty life
　　made so by countless
attempts to fill jars with everything
　　but what mattered.

What is this wet promise you make
　　to me that seems so filling?
O one who sees so deeply into
　　the well of my hiding
dare I drink from such
　　a mysterious fountain?

47

Recall Jesus?

"PETER, YOU HAVE TO talk to him. Even his mother thinks he's crazy." Peter gazed back at John through squinted eyes, "He won't listen to me. You heard what happened last week when I told him how ridiculous this going to Jerusalem to die thing was."

Judas grabbed Peter's shoulder and pushed him around to his direction. "I didn't sign on for this mess. It was bad enough when he picked up that trash Matthew from the tax table and now he's talking about walking extra miles and turning cheeks. The crowds won't put up with this nonsense for too long."

Peter pushed back at Judas sending him toward a nearby olive tree. "Look Judas, this is not some kind of election. The people are fickle. They will follow anybody who promises them something that will make their lives better. I do not know what Jesus has in mind, I just know what I feel when he looks into my eyes."

Judas gave Peter a slight smile, "Looks aren't going to feed people. Looks will not get the Romans off our backs. And this loving enemies stuff is going to do Jesus and us in if he keeps it up."

Jesus seemed to always walk up from nowhere. Now he was standing just behind John. He had some kind of small seeds in his outstretched hand. Jesus stood for a moment just looking at the three disciples. They each wondered if he had overheard their conversation.

Ever so slowly Jesus allowed the seeds to sift through his slightly opened fingers. The wind took some while other seeds fell just beside the feet of the now silent followers. Jesus spoke softly into the night breeze, "You know a seed doesn't do much until it falls to the ground and dies. Once it breaks open in death, then life begins."

Jesus looked toward each of them individually. He turned and walked toward the olive tree and into the night. "See, that's what I am talking about," whispered Judas. "What the heck is that supposed to mean?"

"Judas," Peter responded, "You have to decide if you are going to be a follower or simply one of the group. None of this has been easy from the very beginning."

Judas kicked some dirt over a few of the seeds that were on the ground and walked away. Peter looked into John's face and noticed that his eyes seemed moist. John took his faraway look and stepped toward the fire were the others were preparing to sleep.

Peter's tired body slid down the base of the olive tree. He picked up one of the seeds from the ground and with his finger turned it over a few times in the palm of his hand. The moon was full.

48

How Far from Heaven

Based on John 14

Too distant to that place
where waves pound not
the shore
but still waters
wait
Hearts shudder with fear
beating in a surrounding
darkness that
holds life in a
grip
Into their fear he speaks
words to still
the waters and
loosen the hold even
of death
"Let not your hearts be troubled,"
spills over into
their emptiness
and suddenly there is
a way
Heaven's distance closes
because of one life—
direction is shown
to a place of
many rooms

Heaven is both ready and
and in our midst
because of the
wounded one—
God's child
Peace is given not by
a tired world
but by one who
conquers fear and closes
the distance
Let not your hearts be troubled
for the one who prepares
rooms of rest
is with us
now
Heaven is not far . . .

49

Imago Dei

Clay in the potter's hands—
Dust gathered by the
   gardener who longs
   to bring life out
   of dry bones

Ancient words tell us
We are "imago Dei"
   shaped by the
   image of a God
   who loves to create

Some think we are but
Faces in the crowd—
   given numbers to
   carry about that
   grant us our identity

But to One who whispers—
"You are imago Dei,"
   we are sacred
   faces reflecting
   the face of our Creator

"See my face," the shaping God
Says when we are told to
   look upon each
   other as images of
   the divine who loves

50

A Prodigal Kind of Love

Based on Luke 15:11–32

Travel brochures for far countries
   fill the shopping lists of our minds,
"Give us blank checks now so that
   we can spend our way to happiness."

A reluctant hand puts pen to paper
   and gives us what we should not have,
"I'll send you a postcard and let you know
   how things are going," comes the promise

But the mailbox remains empty
   and a heart is vacant due to lost love
"My child where are you . . . It matters not
   for all I know is you are not here."

Prodigal love is what God feels for us
   when we take our leave without remembering,
"It's ours after all," we say
   Not wanting to wait for distant promises

And so faded travel brochures dot the
   pig pens of our lives, but we get by,
"My arms wait for you my restless child
   always waiting, no questions asked."

There is a prodigal part of each of us
   that gets lost because of our wanting,
But we think it is an old story about someone else
   so we leave Him on the porch ... looking ... waiting ...

51

God's Front Porch

Based on the Parable of "The Prodigal Son"

He stands there with
only broken hearted
memories to keep
him company
His older boy is lost to
his resentment and he too
has left home
while remaining
A lonely father peers down
a narrow road that seems
to lead nowhere—
the road of a son's leaving
But then one daybreak
a silhouette is seen—
a father's dream
but real ... his boy
And from the porch his tired
frame leaps and
he runs toward
his lost, limping child
Surprised, the prodigal can only
listen to underserved
love dispersed by
a father he rejected
And so the front porch
becomes the gateway to a party

thrown by a father
lost in love
It is a resurrection gala for
his son was dead
and now lives
was lost and is found
But the older boy who stayed
at home will not step
on to the front porch
of his father's waiting
The "elder brother" cannot
feel the joy of return
for he is hiding in
his own far country
So God, like that father,
waits on his front
porch looking down
the road and over his shoulder
Looking for children who wander
and children who stay—
longing for homecoming
and waiting . . . always waiting

52

Ephphatha

Based on Jesus' Healing of the Deaf Mute in Mark 7:34

Sighing he spoke it
and chains
fell and bondage
became a
stale word

Ephphatha—from one
whose words
so often were
soft but this
was a shout

A command to be open
and a man's
frozen tongue
melted into
surprised words

But what was unsaid
was that all
of time and life
heard his shout
to be open

Ephphatha—be open
to love
to grow
to risk
to die
to live

53

Creation

Based on the Creation Accounts in Genesis

One day God . . .
Whoops, no day yet . . .
Once upon time
not once upon "a" time—
this was the real thing

So one "time"
Before time
God decided to
make some things—
lots of things

So God leaned back
In a rocking chair
(God made the chair before
God thought about
making some creation)

God thought
And things came about
According to what
came to mind
at the time before time

In order for
God to see what
What was going to happen next

God created some
light to shine on it all

And since God needed
Some "all" for the light
To shine on, God created
some earth and
some sky and some sea

And believe you me
It was "some" earth and
"Some" sky and "some"
sea, better than
anything before

So God rocked back
And forth and started
Singing and when God sang
the song turned into
some moon and stars

God thought that was great
So God took some of the sea
And earth and juggled them
together and laughed
out loud and made fishes

The fishes seemed to enjoy the
Sea so much that God thought it a
Good idea to make some
animals for the land
so they could have names

And then God thought, "Who's
Gonna name my animals?"
So God took a deep breath
and thought
and images of God happened

And God liked it all
Cause it was so good that
God thought that is was time to rest
a while and simply
enjoy Creation

But God's "images" did not
Want to rest because they
Were so full of themselves
that they forgot
who made them

So God said, "Let there be knowledge of Me"
And the images said in wonder
"Who are you?"
and God said, "I am the
one who made you."

And the images laughed because
They knew that they had always
Been and no one needed making
because life was full
of creation

So God put God's face in God's hands
And wept for it hurt to be forgotten
By images with no memories
and floods and rainbows
became stories

But before there were stories
There was a God who created
And who longs still to be
remembered by images
of a divine making

54

Caught to Catch

Based on Matthew 4:18–22

O Divine One who fished
oceans of long ago,
Cast your net again my way
for to be free
I must be held
by a weaving beyond me.

They knew not what lay ahead
when they left nets hanging empty.
People were to be their catch
for you needed
help in drawing in
a drowning world.

And now you call me to step
away from past comforts.
You bid me join in the casting,
but first capture me again
for I long to swim unhindered
so first I must be caught.

55

As Close as Your Next Breath

Between all that is there
is a whisper to
remind us of
the cavern from
which we all came
where the wind
has its birthing

As we step through life we
must listen to
the whisper in
the swirling wind
for in its call
is the hint
of who we are

We are- each of us—God breathed
dust, shaped in the
infinite mystery of
God's joyful imagining—
lifted to the wind
as an offering
of love seeking breath

So- between all that is there
is a whisper to
remind *you* that
the God who gave

you birth as a gift
is always as
   close as your next breath

56

The Forgetting

A Poem of Thanksgiving

My first cry I remember not—
    reaching for the miracle
    called breath I must
have feared the new light
    and fresh was my
    grief of losing the warm
    comfort of my mother's womb—
and I began the forgetting

Somewhere, someplace I stumbled
    forward, risking the
    new adventure of first steps
and there must have been
    some hands not wanting
    and wanting at the same
    time to let me go—
but I remember not

And now there are so many steps
    to take and my
    grasping hands have
amassed so much of life
    and in my gaining
    of it all, somewhere
    I may have lost the memory—
where did it all come from?

O unseen One who remembers
    my first dawn of birth
    and who watched my first steps
I pause now to thank you
    for the life that came
    from Your hands of
    divine imagination—
save me from the forgetting

57

The Shepherd's Valley

Based on Psalm 23

The walls reach up and make
only darkness—
just enough light
to make shadows
that tease
of life
Words echo in that valley—
empty words
that speak of
lost hope
and dreams
that die
But one shadow reaches toward
the wounded
and speaks
words that echo not—
but that seep into
the darkness
"I am the shepherd of
this valley
and I know its
lonely paths
for I have
walked them all
You are not lost though
so it seems—

for this is my
valley not yours
and I will
lead you home"

58

The Work of Doing Nothing

Based on the Story of Mary and Martha in Luke 10:38–42

She does nothing yet
you salute her
My efforts slighted
while she sits
at your feet

Must all the world
wait on you—
Who will then do
all this serving
of which you speak

You call hers the
finest part
But I was the one
who toiled
so she could sit

Yet what is this tiredness
I feel at labor
Must I first simply
sit at your feet
and listen

This work of doing nothing
is strange to me

but in your deep eyes
of love I feel
drawn to kneel
and simply be

59

Beginning Again

Some part of us may wish
to hold on and struggle
for a constant purpose
wrapped tight with
cords of
certainty.
But there comes a whisper
in the night breeze—
"Be ready always to
begin again, for you
are part of Creation's
woven symmetry
of rebirth."
To not let go would mean
to die to life—
But there is one who
walked our dusty paths
and smiles our way
sensing our
resistance.
"I know your need to stay
the same, O child
of nature's longing,
but letting go means
life to you,
forever.
"Once I told you, but now
you need reminding,

for fear hems you
in and so hear me say,
'Behold I make
all things new.'"
Begin again ...

APPENDIX ONE

Preaching What I Practice

A Sermon for All Seasons

YOU MAY HAVE HEARD the expression, "You need to practice what you preach." This last section is my effort to "preach what I practice." I am a "practicing preacher" with a local congregation. What I write in this book comes out of the practice and "praxis" of being a local church pastor.

I have learned through the trials and errors of life that I can be "chief among sinners" when it comes to getting lost while making excellent time. What follows are sermons that I have preached at the church where I presently serve.

Since I have used the Christian year as a compass to help "us slow down" these sermons are selections from those I have preached in each season of the Christian year.

If you are not interested in "hearing" or reading yet another sermon, well, that is why it is listed as an appendix. After all we know full well that we can live without an "appendix." So if you want to "cut this out" feel free to do so. If not, enjoy my efforts to ponder how to slow down as we navigate through the year.

There is a sermon for each "season" and a few thrown in for that season after Pentecost called, "ordinary time." You can be the judge as to how "ordinary" they are. There is one on "being still," one on parenting, another on evil, and one on "faith healing."

Appendix Two

Advent

Making New Year's Resolutions at the End of Time

MATTHEW 24:36–44

I AM ALWAYS PERPLEXED with the scripture readings for the first Sunday in Advent. The readings usually deal with the second coming of Jesus or the end of the world.

Here we are trying to go over our Christmas shopping list and I'm supposed to talk about the end of time. Why bother shopping if everything is going to be wrapped up soon?

This reminds me of the older gentleman who sat down beside a five year old boy who just received a Mickey Mouse Watch. The young lad was winding the watch. Many people listening to me today have never possessed a watch that needed to be wound, but that's another story.

After watching the boy wind the watch the older man, trying to make conversation with the young boy, asked him, "Well, does it tell you the time?" The boy looked up at the man and replied, "No, you have to look at it."

If we look at the time, this first Sunday in the Christian New Year seems to threaten us with the reality that we better get ready because time might be ending just around the corner. Here we thought the words, "He's making a list and checking it twice, gonna find out who's naughty and nice" referred to the jolly old elf when today's scripture implies the words might just be pointing to none other than Jesus.

Why then would I imply that we might want to make some Christian New Year's resolutions if we are facing the possible end of time? Jesus says to be ready because we never know the hour when the end will come. He then tells us to stay awake because the ending will come like a thief that breaks into one's house when everybody is sleeping.

Now this is starting to sound like the "Grinch who Stole Christmas." Remember that scene in Dr. Seuss's wonderful story when the Grinch sneaks into Cindy Lou Who's home and steals Christmas while the "Who" family is sleeping.

Jesus is not Santa Claus nor is he is the Grinch but on this first Sunday of the Christian year he does seem to sound a clear warning to those of us who will listen. Amidst the sound of Jingle Bells and those who would ask us to count down the 12 days of Christmas Jesus says something like,

> Listen up. In the days of Noah they were all going to the malls and shopping till they dropped. People were making merry at various parties and wrapping presents. Remember what happened to them? They all got swept away in the flood. All Noah and his family witnessed 40 days later was a bunch of wrapped presents floating in the flood waters. Do you want that to happen to you?

Jesus is sounding a bit like the Grinch is he not? Why such harsh words here on the beginning of a journey to that time that some call, "the most wonderful time of the year?"

Sounds like Jesus is trying to get our attention. Now if some of you are like me this is when I want to change channels. I was raised on some of this get right with God before its too late kind of religion. The reference to two people in the field with one taken and one left behind might sell a lot of books but it smacks of a fear based religion. Talk of "rapture" and the battle of Armageddon spook some of us who would rather leave such talk to biblical fundamentalists and TV preachers.

What are we to do with such language? I believe we can make our New Year's resolutions in the midst of this end of the world talk because that is exactly what Jesus is trying to get us to do. This talk is not so much offered to scare us as to shake us to make sure we are awake.

Before the sixth century there was not much to do about Christmas. The season that Christians celebrated was called Winter Lent. It began on November 11th with a celebration of St. Martin's day and it ended on January 6th with the celebration of Epiphany. On Epiphany those who had been preparing for baptism by study, fasting, and repentance were baptized. This 40-day season was a time of preparation.

Epiphany day on January 6 included the celebration of Jesus' birth, the coming of the wise men, and the remembrance of Jesus' baptism, which the early Christians saw as the day of Jesus' inauguration as savior of the world.

It was only later that the Eastern Orthodox Church began celebrating a special day in remembrance of a kindly man who used to give gifts to poor children. That day became known as St Nicholas day and was celebrated on December 6. Over the years Advent was shortened, and as we now know Christmas was "lengthened." Somewhere in the midst of all this shuffling of the Christian year Thomas Moore wrote a poem called, "It Was the Night Before Christmas," and the rest is history.

My job today is not to read, "The Night Before Christmas," nor is it to recite the poetic words of "The Grinch that Stole Christmas." My task is simply to help us rescue Advent from the Christmas rush. As one writer put it, "Can Christians regain custody of Christmas?"

Could this be part of Jesus warning? In shortening Advent and lengthening Christmas have we thrown out the baby with the bathwater?

Why are books like "The DaVinci Code," "The Gnostic Gospels," and even the "Left Behind" series so popular? There are many reason but I think one is that many of us are seeking the "secret." There must be something more to religion than meets the eye. There must be a hidden code that only some can see.

The old word for this is *gnosis*. *Gnosis* is the word for special knowledge that is given by God to those who seek revelation. In a world that has become frightening and complicated we long to know that there is special revelation that will tell us the secret of life.

This thinking leads to some wanting to be ruptured out of the world while others are left behind. Others who seek this special knowledge long to find the secret truth about things that the church hides about the life and love life of Jesus assuming that the company line that the church offers is not sufficient.

Actually the word used in the phrase "one in the field will be taken and one will be left" refers more to the idea of being taken in not taken out. Jesus is talking about those who "get it" and those who do not get it because they are asleep to the reality of the present Kingdom of God in their midst.

Those who wake up and get it hear Jesus say, "I'm quite taken with you for your watchfulness." These people are saved only to be used. Jesus is not offering some secret code or knowledge nor is he trying to predict the end of time. He is saying that every day matters because it is a day to do the work of the kingdom. Time is always short.

So many books tell of the time of the end. Jesus clearly says that no one knows that time. Jesus is not so much offering a chronological time line as he is offering an internal change of time and mind.

It seems that the Jesus' words convey that he just might want to break into our lives and shout, "Wake up, pay attention for heavens' sake. Yes, there is global warming. Yes, too many children are dying. Yes, you need to learn how to get along without killing each other. Yes, you are using up the world's resources like you think it is yours to use up. Wake up. Don't be left behind when it comes to offering the kingdom of God to a world that is asleep."

In Kenya recently a saintly man was buried. The whole village turned out to pay respects to Zacharias. A visitor to the village who attended the funeral out of courtesy was walking beside a young girl. He asked about Zacharias because he could tell how much the villagers loved him. The young girl smiled and said that Zacharias died, *Ki-sabuni*.

"What do you mean by *Ki-sabuni*," the man asked? The girl said that *Ki-sabuni* was Swahili for "like a bar of soap."

> *Ki-subuni*. You know. In the house, the bar of soap sits next to the basin, available morning, noon, and night to all- the children, adults, the elderly, family, and guests alike. It never discriminates or complains of being used and reused. It is taken for granted as it slowly disappears, until someone exclaims, "gosh the soap is gone." Zacharias was that kind of man.[1]

Jesus could have told the parable of the bar of soap. He might say we are saved to be used. We are not "taken" so that we will be lifted out of the world but we are taken that we might be used.

Jesus warns us today not so much to frighten us but to remind us that the end is always near. We never know. Every day is a day to be awake.

Remember the feeling of the teacher saying, "Times' up put down your pencils?" This meant that the test was over. There was no more time to write what you had learned. As we face this season before us and as we look into another Christian year Jesus says to us "time is almost up." But take heart we do have some more time to take this test.

---

1. Healy, *Once Upon a Time in Africa*, 23.

Advent is still for those who wish to observe it as a time of warning and preparation. It is a time to wake up and change direction. It is a time to be saved that we can live *ki-sabuni*. May you and I live so long that we are not just "worn out" but may we live so faithfully that we are "used up" like a bar of soap. Sounds like a good New Year's resolution to me.

APPENDIX THREE

A Christmas Sermon

What Kind of Jesus Are You Expecting?

LUKE 3:7–18

SOME PEOPLE ARE STILL getting over my "dirty diapers" Christmas Eve sermon of a couple of years ago including one of my daughters and my wife. "You could have done without that," was the comment. Perhaps I did as I have done before. I overshot the point. The point was, "How real is Jesus to you? Is he real enough to think that just maybe Mary and Joseph had to change his diapers?"

Okay, maybe so but can't we leave stuff like that out of church talk especially at Christmas when we want to think about angel songs and a baby Jesus who according to one beloved carol is one who "no crying he makes." Well if you have trouble with this kind of stunning reality I just want you to know that I stand in the tradition of the guy who is the publicity agent for the child born in a manger.

How about this for a Christmas greeting card:

"You brood of vipers! Who warned you to flee the wrath to come? You come out here to hear about the good news of a savior who is coming but I tell you the fact that you are a card carrying church goer is no big deal to God. Do not focus on the dirty people out there in the world, you church people need to get clean first. By the way, Merry Christmas."

As we approach Christmas just what kind of Jesus are you expecting to find? The people who come out into the desert to hear John advertise about a coming savior have three basic expectations. They want either a new king who will get rid of the present administration and put a chicken in every pot and bread on the table or they want a new priestly leader who will finally make the church of the day relevant to real life instead of all the empty ritual that seems like dust in their mouths, or finally they want an angelic, "apocalyptic" figure who will swoop down from the sky and with some kind of magic wand get rid of evil things like Pilate, and Herod, and Rome . . . and maybe my manipulative mother-in-law.

It looks as if even Jesus' agent gets it wrong. John seems to want a savior who will "lay the ax to the root of the tree" and do some heavy pruning. John wants a Messiah who will clean house and restore purity to the religion of the day. We know that John is a bit disappointed because some months later when he is arrested by Herod and put in prison, John sends some of his own followers to ask Jesus, "Are you really the one I advertised or do we need to keep looking?"

Jesus sends word back to John,

> I'm the one John. I'm just not exactly the one you wanted but don't feel too alone because I'm not the one a lot of people want, including some of the folks listening to the sermon at Davidson United Methodist Church this morning. Some of them want me to be a magician of sorts who will snap my fingers and fix bad things for them. Others of them want me to be a kind of distant hero who they can come to and nod to once in a while at church but who will leave them alone when it comes to politics or money. There are some sitting in church today, John, who want me to a combination of Santa Claus and a kind of old, gentle king sitting on a throne. I'm none of those, John, but I am the real savior.

John may be wrong about some things just like we are with our hopes and expectations but John is right when the people ask him, "Well what are we to do to get ready for this coming savior?" The word, "do" is better translated, "What are we to bare?" It has to do with what a tree "does." A tree "bares" fruit or it is not good for keeping. It is cut down and thrown into the fire, so says John.

So on our shopping list for Christmas according to John we have the following:—The first thing is that if we have we must share. It is not an option for the one who wants to be a follower of the new way of life. If you have two coats share one with someone who does not have a coat."— The next two things John puts on the Christmas shopping list have to do with contentment and "being satisfied with what you have." He tells the tax collectors to not be so greedy and he tells some soldiers in the crowd who would have probably been some of Herod's hired thugs to not extort people just because they could. In those days a soldier had the right to ask about anything he wanted of someone and they had to comply. In other words the way this translates for us today is just because we can do something because we have the money or the power does not mean that we should do it.

I am reading a book now entitled, "How to Want What You Have: Discovering the Magic and Grandeur of Ordinary Existence." Timothy Miller writes that the systemic problem we have as human beings in our culture is that we instinctively want "more." He does studies on human instinct and discovers that the drive to want more is inbred in human beings. The word "enough" is not part of the instinctive dictionary.

Studies show that once basic survival needs are meet that the human being does not become happier with more stuff. People with "more" after basic needs are meet are simply not happier because they have more. They always want a little bit more.

Miller says the secret is ancient. One must learn to recognize this craving for more and get hold of it by learning about the "precious present." He offers three patterns to curb the instinctual habit of always wanting a little bit more. These patterns revolve around three basic principles: Compassion, Attention, and Gratitude. Each principal approaches the task of wanting what you have so that we will not always try to have what we want . . . and crave more.[1]

Compassion is "the intention to see each human being as no better or worse than yourself, neither more nor less important, and as fundamentally similar to yourself." I think this principal helps us understand that when Jesus is asked in what measure we will be judged to see if we are really following him he says, "It is based on the way you treat the least of these because they are fundamentally like you."[2]

The second principal to help us want what we have rather than always trying to have what we want is Attention. Attention is "the intention to avoid unnecessary value judgments about your own experience . . . to live without reservation in the here and now."

Gratitude is the third principal. Gratitude is the intention to count your blessings every day, even every minute, while avoiding the belief that

1. Miller, *How to Want What You Have*, 2.

2. Ibid, 16.

you need or deserve different circumstances."[3] Compassion, Attention, and Gratitude are wonderful ways to understand John's shopping list, which include sharing and being content with what we have.

The story today says that "the people were filled with expectation." Okay let's stop right now and check our "expectation meter." Are we so preoccupied with Christmas past or some hoped for Christmas future that we are missing the precious present? After all, the baby Jesus in our manger scene is the same one that we pulled out of the box last year. We know what to expect, but just maybe we are like so many in John and Jesus' own day. Maybe we are wrong. Maybe we no longer expect anything new to happen at Christmas. We get caught in longings and wanting "something more."

We sing "Come Thou Long Expected Jesus" but we do not have much spirit behind the words. John may have been wrong in his hoping that the savior would topple governments and set up a new church administration but he was right about what the baby born in a manger really wants to bring. John says that although water baptism is a good reminder that church folks need to clean up our act, that the one coming will "baptize you with the Holy Spirit and with fire."

Anybody "on fire" this morning? Remember what the man said about the employer who was concerned about the poor performance of an employee: "You seemed concerned that your employee is acting like he is burned out. That can't be true because in my opinion he was never on fire to begin with."

Hey brood of vipers, the baby is coming not so that we can sing carols. The baby is coming to change the world. How is he going to do this? He will do it one person at a time. It is the same way you and I change the world, one person at a time beginning with our willingness to show compassion, to pay attention, and feel gratitude.

What kind of Jesus are you expecting this Christmas? Have we quit expecting?

The one who comes is the one with fire and a winnowing fork in his hand, but the fire is not to burn us up but to purify us. What needs to be burned up for you today? In my life there are some old patterns that revolve around having and possessing that need some fire. There may be for you some self doubts and self image things that need to be burned up.

3. Ibid, 17.

The winnowing fork is to help us separate the wheat from the chaff. How much of what we do is pointless. I know I need to offer this savior some of my worry and let him sift it for me and let it go with the wind.

Christmas begins with us as individuals but it is given in order to be shared with the world. Compassion, Attention, and Gratitude help remind us that the long expected Jesus is the one who offers us a way of life centered in living in the precious present so that we can feel love and share it.

Let me share what happened to me the other day which reminded me that Christmas is an expectation that begins with the individual but which must be shared with the world. Here is what I wrote after "it" happened:

SEEING CHRISTMAS, AGAIN

The other afternoon I was feeling a little lost. Being a minister at Christmas is like jumping onto a fast moving train that is speeding toward Bethlehem. You know the destination because you have been there many times before. The tracks are stationary but everything is going so fast. Everybody on the train seems to be longing for something really special to happen but you know that the destination is the same as it is every year and you wonder just what you can do to make it "really special" this year for those on the train who look to you with a kind of Christmas longing in their eyes.

I decided to go watch Christmas for "me." The movie, "The Nativity" was showing at the theatre so I bought my ticket for the 5 o'clock show. Running a bit late having had to jump the fast train, I wondered how much of the "birth" I had missed. As I opened the door to the dark theatre Bethlehem came into view. There was no star shinning yet but the ray of light from the back of the room allowed me to find my seat.

I could not believe what I saw. There was no one else in the theatre. I was alone in Bethlehem. To tell you the truth it felt good. There would be no crowds, no expectation of me to make sure the story would come alive and make a difference. Somehow this felt like a Christmas gift. I was going to be able to watch the Christmas story just for me.

I could almost hear a still small voice whisper, "Have a seat Jody. This is your own private screening of a story that you have offered to so many others. Have a seat and enjoy it for yourself."

The Bethlehem scene that began the movie was a flashback. I had not missed the birth. I watched as a frightened but obedient teenage girl tried to explain an unplanned pregnancy to both her father and mother and to an older fiancé who seemed to be both very much in love with this little girl and who was extremely broken hearted at her betrayal. Joseph's struggle to both want to hate her and love her came to life in the solitary darkness.

He "would not make an accusation," he tells a brokenhearted mother and father. Joseph goes to his home and all alone with me in that theatre he has a sweaty dream. He brushes aside the blanket and looks up into what he thinks is a blinding light that disappears like the dew that is his dream. "Is it real. Is it real? O God is it real?"

Those words do not come from the screen. I find myself saying them. I'm putting words in Joseph's mind and mouth. I know where the train is going but suddenly all alone in the darkness I am part of the story.

Well, the story ended the way I knew it would. There were wise men and there were shepherds who stumbled down a hill late at night to discover that voices from the night sky were in fact real. There was a brutal king who was willing to kill every male child in Bethlehem to assure that the truth would not be alive.

And there was a kind of mystical light shining on a young girl's face who held a tiny infant. I thought the movie was going to end with a collage I have put together many times. Wise men knelt with nearby shepherds still marveling at what was happening. But it did not end there.

A still tired Joseph and Mary responded to yet another dream and find themselves in the desert leading to Egypt fleeing the wrath of a world that does not want any God to "do it this way." The last scene is the silhouette of a "holy family" running away from hate. As the credits start to roll I remember the train and realize that it will stop only for a while in Bethlehem for it will roll into Jerusalem later and the hate will catch up with the child in the form of a cross.

O what a gift to sit alone in a theatre and watch the story for myself. I walked out into the cool night air and jumped back onto the train. I knew where it was going but I must admit I felt some new excitement about getting there. Maybe it all starts with being "alone" with the one who gives the story. I know it does not end there for there is much to do in a broken world to offer healing, but it sure felt wonderful to begin again with the nativity.

A Christmas Monologue Sermon

"The Adopted Father"

A MONOLOGUE BASED ON MATTHEW 1:18–24

I WISH YOU COULD have heard how he answered their questions. Twelve years old and he spoke as one who had mastered the many scrolls of our laws. He spoke of the words of the prophets not like they were distant proclamations of former heroes. He recited their words like they were words from his family members at some gathering that he had attended.

The looks on the faces of those learned men in the Temple were priceless. As I listened to him respond to their questions, I realized that some of the questions were asked in hope that one would make him finally stumble. Suddenly one of the scribes blurted out, "Who is this boy and where is his father?" I proudly raised my hand and spoke,

"I am his father. His name is Jesus and we are from Nazareth."

"Nazareth," responded the scribe, "How can this boy know so much if he was raised in Nazareth? I know the Rabbi in Nazareth and it is impossible that he could have taught your Jesus this much in such a short time."

"He's always been very bright." I smiled as I said those words.

Then I left him to continue his discussion. As I walked away to join Mary and the others I could only imagine what these scholars of our scriptures must be thinking as they listened to him speak of things beyond what any child could make up.

So it was that I was most embarrassed two days later when we were returning from Jerusalem to Nazareth after the festival. I assumed that Jesus was with some of my family. He was becoming hard to keep up with.

He was beginning to spend more and more time away from us and Mary and I knew that it was approaching that time that we would have to let him go his way.

When Mary asked me if I had seen him I said "no" but that I was sure he must be with Simon or Benjamin's family. Our search revealed no Jesus.

We turned and walked back to Jerusalem. I knew where to go. I found Jesus on the Temple steps again discussing some interpretation of one of the scrolls with those baffled priests and scribes. I listened for a moment as he expounded on some words from the scroll of Isaiah about the role of the suffering servant in God's plan to save the people.

It was then that I interrupted, "Son, you have caused much worry for your mother. Why did you not come when summoned?"

Jesus looked my way with eyes that seemed almost confused. His response did indeed confuse those who had been listening so intensely as this upstart boy interpreted ancient words; "Did you not know that I must be about my father's business?"

As he lowered his head and obediently walked over to me one of the scribes said, "I thought you were his father?" I started to respond to him but I knew there were no words that could contain any explanation. I simply looked down into "my son's" face as he smiled my way, reached for my arm, and said, "I am sorry father. I hope you understand?"

"Father," the sound of the word still echoes in my memory. These carpenter hands have crafted so many things, but the finest thing in my life I did not make. I am an adopted father.

I loved her from the moment I first saw her drawing water from the well at the edge of Nazareth. I did not want to grow old alone. I wanted children. The people of Nazareth all treated me with respect and none of them knew the deep longings that dwelt within my heart.

After all, I was Joseph the carpenter who made their tables, chairs, and the cradles for their children. I was the elder who was often asked to read the scriptures in our synagogue. Me not being married was to them a sign of my independence and strength. Perhaps I had given myself to my work and my role as leader of our village so much that "Joseph did not need the love of a woman nor did he need children who would sleep in his cradle."

They were wrong. So it surprised some when I signed the contract of betrothal with Mary's father. I paid the customary amount to her father to acquire her. Mary was there for the blessing of the contract. The Rabbi said the ancient words. Mary looked up at me only once. It was a look of respect. How I wanted so much more from her deep eyes but what could I expect. She was the property of her father and she was simply there to complete an arrangement. She would remain in her father's house until that day of our wedding.

Mary and I would take walks near her home. I told her that our wedding would be a gala event and I promised to provide a good life for her or at least as good as one could expect in our poor village. Mary would only nod and try to smile. She said very little to me and since I was so much older she treated me more as a father than as one who would be her husband.

How I wished there was more in her heart for me. I made an arrangement, but what I desired was a relationship. Mary knew that she was betrothed to a man who was respected and who was a leader, but I wanted something other than respect for a man who was seen as righteous and upright. No one knew these feelings of mine but God and me.

Ah, God, there is where things get complicated. I will never forget the day Mary came to me in the early morning. It was not acceptable for her to come to my house unaccompanied so I was surprised to see her. She stood in my doorway as the new day's sunlight came over her shoulders. The morning light behind her made her look radiant but then she always looked radiant to me.

As she stepped my way I could tell that she had been crying. I wanted to comfort her but we were still only acquaintances and the marriage was months off. I lived in the hope that she would learn to at least want to love me. Her next words almost stopped my longing heart, "Joseph, I do not know what words to use to tell you this. I am with child."

Hearts break in many ways. Mine was already wounded from too many years of being alone. Now my Mary had ended all hopes for a future, a future with someone who would fill my solitude, even if it was an arrangement.

After the pain came the fear, fear for her. I knew what our scrolls of the law said. Such an act of adultery by a virgin who was betrothed was an abomination. According to the scroll of Deuteronomy, I was to report the act to her father who then had the option of taking her to the gates of our Nazareth and having her stoned to death by the village elders for the sin. My Mary, an abomination! I wondered if Mary even knew of the words of our ancient law. She was so young and of course being a woman was not allowed to hear the words of the law that were read by people like me in the synagogue.

I knew my other choice was to negotiate with her father. I could ask him to keep the money that I had paid for Mary's betrothal and convince him to use that part of it to arrange a private divorce. I could then ask him to take Mary from Nazareth for a while so she could have the child away from the stares and the whispers that would surely come.

I was lost in this dialogue within my mind when Mary reached her hand out to me and placed it against my arm:

> O Joseph, it is not what you think. One evening weeks ago the light of our God overwhelmed me and a voice said to me that I would be the mother of the Messiah. I told this messenger that I had not yet been with you, but the voice said to me that God's spirit would do this. I do not know why God chose me Joseph. I am both filled with fear and joy at the same time. I am sorry, Joseph, for I cannot expect you to understand.

She then turned and walked away into the morning. I wanted to be angry. I wanted to scream at how cruel all of this was. Had I not tried to be faithful and patient? What kind of message must this be from God? I could not imagine my Mary being with someone else but then I knew the impossibility of what she was saying. Somehow anger could not find a place in me. I believe it was because there was so much love for Mary within me that there simply was no room for anger.

The next few nights were sleepless. All I could think of were the words I would need to put together to explain to Mary's father what needed to done so that Mary could escape as much pain was possible. I knew that because of my role in our village that I could convince her father that my decision to privately divorce her would be best for the family. I would not allow him to act on his sense of betrayal by his daughter. Stones of judgment would have to remain on the ground.

Somehow I managed to sleep that one evening. It was a restless sleep. I smile now as I think of that night and I remember how our ancestor Jacob wrestled with his angel. After that encounter by the river Jabbok, Jacob's life and name were changed. After my encounter this night my life was forever changed.

The voice punctured my wall of fear and betrayal. At first I it was almost like the piercing words from Mary's announcement telling me that she was going to have a child that was not mine. The words this time though were haunting. "Do not be afraid to take Mary as your wife, Joseph. The child is mine." "The child is mine?" "What does that mean, I said to the darkness?" "Whose child is this? Mine, who is mine?" "I wanted 'mine' to be mine."

I realized even in my dream-like state my words made no sense. None of this made any sense.

Then there came the silence, the deep silence. The silence was penetrating like the look in Mary's eyes. The silence spoke words. Do not ask me to explain this. I then knew what I was to do.

"How could this be," no longer mattered. I simply knew it was true.

This time I surprised Mary and her parents with my visit. I was allowed by custom to request to be alone with Mary. Her father quickly granted my request. I could tell by his manner that he did not yet know of Mary's news.

Mary walked beside me but she would not look at me. We walked in silence for a while. I took her to the well where I first saw her. No one else was there.

> Mary you were not aware of the first time I saw you draw water from this well. As I looked at your innocence I knew I wanted and needed you. For months I waited and then arranged for us to be betrothed. You are mine, Mary.

She looked down into the darkness of the well. I reached toward her chin and gently lifted her eyes to mine:

> I am not talking property rights, Mary. I do not care about the legal arrangement or the customs. You are mine, Mary, because of my love for you. You are mine because I need your love.

It was only then that she looked up. I did not allow her to ask a question.

> I found my angel last night Mary, or did my angel find me? I know I am not the father, Mary, but I know who the father is. Mary, can I be our son's adopted father?

Then her eyes looked not at me but into me. Her tears came first. She then did what I had only dreamed of her doing. She leaned into my chest and slowly put her arms around my shoulders. She said nothing for a few long moments. I could only feel her gentle sobs.

Then she leaned back and looked at me. She cupped my face in her soft hands and said, "O my Joseph, how I will need you. Our son needs a father."

Words cannot hold meaning sometimes. Her words were so full that the meaning broke open. No vessel could contain what she tried to say. Her words, "O my Joseph" were words that filled my ache and my longing, and those words, "Our son needs a father" completed my life.

I took Mary to my home as was allowed by our custom. Her pregnancy then became acceptable and the whispers had to be put in their place.

In the evenings after I finished my work I would put my head on Mary's swelling abdomen. I watched the movement of what must be a knee or an arm. I smiled as she winced at such play within her.

When I told her of the news that I would have to return to Bethlehem because the hated Romans had again declared that we must register for more taxes or face the consequences, Mary announced that she was going with me. I told her that there was no way she could manage such a three-day journey in her condition.

In a family the husband's word should be the final word, but you do not know my Mary. She looked at me and said that she could not be without me no matter what. She said this must somehow be part of God's plan. I can deal with God on one hand and Mary on the other hand, but I cannot manage both God and Mary.

That was it and I knew it. It took us five days to make the journey to Bethlehem because we had to stop so much. Her pain was becoming something that had to be listened to.

We arrived late in the evening. By this time Mary was holding onto our tired burros' neck and leaning into her pain. As I negotiated with the innkeeper who kept telling me that sleeping space was long since occupied, I pointed to Mary's condition.

He shook his head in wonder and motioned for me to follow him.

> Look, my wife died a few years ago. I have no one to send back here to help you and your wife through this. I will bring you water and some cloth. That is the best that I can do. This is indeed a God forsaken time.

I thanked him. Mary looked up at me through her pain and then around at the animals in the stable. She managed a smile and only said, "God is full of surprises is he not, my Joseph?" "Yes, Mary," I said, "I suppose you and I should be used to being surprised by now."

The innkeeper brought me the promised water, some strips of cloth, and a lantern. As he turned to walk away I simply said to him, "After tonight this time will not be so God forsaken." He looked back at me and nodded. I knew he did not understand my words but then who would be able to understand any of this?

Mary's labor was not long but it was hard. I did not know what to do but I did it. Men were not supposed to do such things. It was ritually unclean for me to help with childbirth, but then this was not an ordinary evening. If I could not be there in the making of our child I was to be there at his birth.

He was born early in the morning before the sun came up. I wrapped him in the bands of cloth I had cut and handed him to Mary. Her swollen face smiled at me and at him as she nursed him. There can be no more precious sight than a mother nursing a child, especially this child. She then gently rocked him in her arms. His eyes closed.

The night was still and the animals seemed to act as quiet a witness to the moment that was to change everything. Then Mary looked up at me, "Joseph, here is your son." She handed him to me and we shared a knowledge that no one else could share.

His eyes opened ever so slightly and he looked at me.

"I take you as my son O little one, though you are not of my making."

As I laid him in the manger close by, I looked down at Mary who was trying to rest in the place where one of the cows had been sleeping.

I looked down into the manger and said to our son, "Your name shall be Jesus. A father always names the child." And then I looked toward Mary and then toward Jesus and said, "O child of mystery, your father gave me your name one evening in my dreams and though that father shall always be yours so shall I be your father also."

I heard a noise behind me and noticed a group of shepherds walking toward us. I wondered what they must want.

Mary reached up to me with a woven garment that she had next to her,

Dear Joseph thank you for listening to your dreams. I need you to be a father to our Jesus for I sense in my heart that his other father has much for our child to do some of which already causes fear to well up in me. For now take this blanket and cover him Joseph, the night is growing cold.

Appendix Five

Epiphany: The Baptism of the Lord

Remembering That We are Remembered

S HE STOOD IN THE doorway holding it in her hand, tears slowly edging down her face. Her only words were, "You remembered, I thought you had forgotten."

It was Thanksgiving evening sixteen years ago. The woman crying was my mother. She held in her hands the reason for the tears. On the folded pieces of notebook paper were words penned by our oldest daughter, Abigail. Abigail had shared with me what she created for an essay she was required to write in her high school English class on the assigned theme of "the person who has influenced you the most."

Abigail wrote about her childhood memories of being held in such a special light by her grandmother. She wrote of sitting on her knee and listening to "Fly Little Blue Bird Through my Garden," and "Itsy Bitsy Spider, Crawling Up the Wall." Her essay contained vivid memories of my mother buying many more panty hose than she would ever use just so she could take the plastic eggs that the "Leggs" hose came in and then filling them with tiny toys that Abigail loved.

There were words that portrayed the many famous, "Granny Breakfasts" that my mother would make for Abigail. Shoney's breakfast buffet was nothing compared to the variety and magnitude of the table my mother set for her first grandchild. More than once Abigail ate so much that she got sick from overeating.

Then Abigail would watch her grandmother wrap her hair in some strange looking foam-rubber device that assured her perfectly styled hair would not be spoiled. They would then pile into the back bed in the main bedroom in our two-bedroom house and watch "The Dukes of Hazard" and whatever else Abigail would choose. It did not matter if my Dad and Abigail's grandfather wanted to watch something else on the only TV in our house. When Abigail was present my Dad's wishes for anything were far in the background.

Abigail requested that I proofread her essay. What she wrote brought tears to my eyes. The one thing I remember is telling my wife Betsy that the way it was written was in a style that almost presumed my mom was gone. I told Betsy, "We need to let Mom read this before something happens. This is too good for her to miss."

My mother was not a well person. She had battled illness most of her adult life, but she was not that sick, I thought.

So it was that on Thanksgiving evening of Abigail's junior year in High School that my mother left the room where we were eating and read Abigail's tribute. Abigail was at the age that grandchildren get. It was no longer cool to go to Granny's house. Abigail had her friends, which took priority. Why it was barely cool to hang around her own house too long.

I could tell that it hurt Mom's feelings that neither Abigail nor her sister Amanda, younger by four years, found all kinds of excuses not to go the Granny and Paw Paw's. This essay filled in spaces that were vacant for years.

And then those words came as she looked through tears at the young woman that little child she held on her knee had become, "You remembered, I thought you had forgotten," were some of her final words.

You must know this morning that the reason this very special memory is at the top of our family's snap shots of the past is that later that night, very unexpectedly, my 67 year old mother slumped over and died in that same chair in which she held her grandchildren and sang "Fly Little Blue Bird."

When my father called me late that night in shock to tell me the tragic news the first thing I said to Betsy was, "My God, we had a going away party and we did not even know it." "You remembered. I thought you had forgotten."

Today is the Baptism of the Lord Sunday when we are called to remember our own baptisms. Many of us here today do not remember our baptism because the sacred waters touched our heads while we were infants. So every time I baptize a child I pour the blessed waters and say to all of us gathered, "Remember your baptism and be grateful."

But what I want to remind you of today is even more basic. I want you to remember that you are remembered. God never forgets the day of your baptism. As life gets less child-like and more complicated and even hard and sometimes cruel we may utter words toward our heavenly parent like, "You remembered, I thought you had forgotten."

Do we forget our baptism because there are consequences for remembering it? Are we like the little five year old girl who, having been baptized the Sunday before, went to her father as they prepared to go to church the following Sunday and said, "Hey let's take Tommy and get him advertised too."

Being baptized in the name of Christ is to live into being an advertisement for the Christian faith. In our baptism we are claimed by God and commissioned for discipleship in the name of Christ. One person put it this way; we are to grow up into our baptism so that we can let our "baptism really happen to us" in the now.

Like Jesus' own baptism, the skies need to open "for us" and we need to hear that "we" are beloved by God and that because we are claimed as God's own, God is pleased with "us." Knowing who we are and whose we are we then have to decide what "role" our baptism calls us to live.[1]

Mark's story of Jesus is believed to be the first gospel written. It is often called a gospel of immediacy because Mark uses the adverb "immediately" 42 times. There is an urgency of words and tone in Mark. The literal translation of the text says that, "As Jesus was coming up out of the waters he immediately saw the heavens torn apart and he immediately heard, 'You are my chosen I am well pleased.'"

Today is one of those immediate moments of urgency. I had an urgency to let my mother know that Abigail remembered. I could not explain that urgency but if Abigail had not shared that remembrance with mom on that particular Thanksgiving evening she would have missed being remembered.

Today is a special day when we are urged to remember our baptism. We are asked to remember and to live into our baptism. God has chosen us in our baptism. God never takes back that closeness. God always

---

1. McGowan, *Textweek Online.*

remembers, but do we remember? I know I often times live like I have forgotten my baptism.

I act like ignorance is bliss. I do not have to forgive enemies, strive for peace with justice for the little ones of life, share my possessions rather than hoard them. I can live for myself for I forget the one who chooses me . . . I forget the one who chooses me . . . always.

To be baptized is to be claimed by something and someone bigger than you. As a man in AA once said, "I promised to quit drinking at the bottom of every bottle. It never worked until I handed the remote to God."

There are many things we have freedom to do and to choose, but to be a disciple of the one who stood in line to be baptized with us is to give some control to him. As long as we have the remote we will choose not to do those hard tasks of discipleship and we will not give up those things that keep us living as we are living now.

One of my favorite new hymns, "You Are Mine" says it this way:

> I will come to you in the silence
> I will lift you from all your fear
> Listen to my voice, I claim you as my choice
> Be still and know that I am here.
> Do not be afraid I am with you,
> I have called you each by name,
> Come and follow me, I will lead you home,
> I love you and you are mine.[2]

Every year I need to "re up" when it comes to my baptismal vows. I will tell you the reason I need to do that. My heart becomes restless, my loyalties and priorities become scattered. I have made promises to people and to God that I have broken. I have forgotten again the haunting words of Bob Dylan's song, "You're Gonna Serve Somebody:"

> You may be an ambassador to England or France
> You may like to gamble; you might like to dance,
> You may be the heavyweight champion of the world,
> You may be a socialite with a long string of pearls,
> But you're gonna serve somebody, yes indeed,
> You're gonna serve somebody.
> Well, it may be the devil or it may be the Lord,
> But you're gonna serve somebody.[3]

2. Hass, *"You Are Mine."*

3. Dylan, "Gotta Serve Somebody." *Gotta Serve Somebody*. Sony, 2003.

We may act like we forget our vows of baptism. We may live like we serve somebody other than the Lord whose name we were baptized into but the one who stood in line for us to be baptized in the Jordan river by John and his heavenly father who told him that day he was the chosen and the beloved one, never forgets our baptism.

So perhaps today we can look toward Jesus and his father and we can whisper to one another, "You remembered, I thought you had forgotten." This is another one of those moments of immediacy because each day is the beginning and each day can be our end as my mother discovered.

This week we buried Betsy's mother and I heard again the words I share with you today:

As in baptism Francis put on Christ so may Francis now be clothed with glory.

It is time to begin again. It is time to remember our baptism. It is time to remember our baptism and be grateful.

Appendix Six

Transfiguration: God's Extreme Makeover
The Transfiguration of the Lord

MATTHEW 17:1–9

ANYBODY HERE EVER BEEN cut from an athletic team? It is not a good feeling. I made the cut when it came to high school football so I thought I would give it shot at the basketball team. Many of my friends were on the team and I thought it would be a good way to get some dates. Besides the uniforms were cool.

The fact that I was not that good at basketball did not deter either Stanley Berkshire, the split end on the football team or me. We thought we might have an inside track because the head basketball coach was our assistant coach in football. He liked Stanley and me.

To our buddies' surprise Stanley and I survived the first few cuts. The squad was down to the final cut. Two others had to go to get the team down to the required number.

After an especially hard practice we were all headed down to the locker room when the words came from coach Graham. "Could I see Berkshire and Seymour for a few minutes." My "buddies" all looked at us as we walked over toward the coach and they started down the stairs toward the showers.

One of my close friends started smiling and doing a slashing motion across his neck as he walked off the court. Everyone knew what was going to transpire. Stanley and I knew what was coming.

Stanley was a funny guy. He was the one I told you about in another sermon who stood up in the back of my typing class one day when I was having an altercation with my typing teacher. Stanley shouted, "Hit her Seymour, hit her." I later ended up in the guidance counselor's office confronted with why I hit Miss Cox. Of course I did not hit her but the word got out because of Stanley's remark that I had.

Stanley in only the way Stanley could, looked over at the coach as we walked away from the others and offered that famous laugh of his framed with the words, "I guess this is the death walk huh coach?" Don Graham was a nice guy. He attended church at Salem Lutheran church where the girl I was dating attended. Coach knew both of us well and this was hard for him.

He started the usual stuff about how hard we had practiced and how much he appreciated our contribution. Stanley and I had discussed this moment ahead of time because we knew our talent potential, we knew the other guys on the team, and we knew it was just a matter of time before the ax would fall.

At the same moment we blurted out in the middle of his sentence, "We quit, you don't have to fire us." We laughed a good laugh and shook good old Don Graham's hand. He smiled at us and walked away.

I wonder what those other disciples thought when Jesus said, "I need to see James, John, and Peter for a few minutes after practice?" Jesus then walked away from the other nine disciples and took these three disciples up on a nearby mountain. Who made the "cut?" Did Matthew, Judas, Thomas, and the others figure they were in or out? Was Jesus taking these three away because they were in and the others were out or was it the other way around?

The reason such a concern was salient to these followers of Jesus was because of the first words we hear in the text for today. It says, "Six days later Jesus took with him Peter, James, and John and led them up to a high mountain." Six days after what? It was evidently six days after Peter publicly confessed that Jesus was in fact the long awaited deliverer.

This was wonderful for a few shining moments until Jesus announced that this meant that he had to go to Jerusalem and be murdered by the government and church in order to pull this off. Peter then took Jesus on and informed Jesus on behalf of the other dumbfounded disciples that they had not signed on for a suicide mission and they wanted nothing of this winning by loosing thing.

Jesus' response to Peter echoes through the ages, "Get thee behind me Satan. You speak for the easy way. I'm taking the road less traveled." After such an altercation no wonder the disciples were wondering "six days later" just who was going to make the cut when it came to this discipleship, cross, and death thing.

What happens next is called the Transfiguration. Simply put Jesus has an extreme makeover to get him ready to make his hard trip to Jerusalem. The story tells us his body began to glow and he was changed before the three disciples' eyes into a radiant, divine like figure. To put icing on the cake and make sure the disciples realized that this is no ordinary day nor an ordinary Jesus, Moses and Elijah, who have been dead for centuries, show up to hob knob with Jesus.

Extreme makeovers are in these days. The reality TV show "Extreme Makeover" in which individuals are given all sorts of plastic surgery treatments is a real hit. So much so that ABC now has a "home version" of the show in which an entire house receives an extreme makeover. The FOX channel's has copied this idea in their show called "the Swan" in which women are made over with everything from nose jobs to tummy tucks to front end enhancements; and then placed up against each other in a bizarre kind of beauty contest.

The truth is on this mount of Transfiguration it is a day for an extreme makeover. Jesus evidently does need some alteration but it is not the kind of alteration that a surgeon's scalpel can achieve. Jesus needs the shaping hand of his father to grab hold of him and offer him whatever it is going to take to deliver the people.

Jesus hears in his altered state words of encouragement from God. "You are my son, my beloved." The use of the word "beloved" calls to mind the name, "David," which means "beloved of God." This shinning figure on the mountain will be known as the "son of David," but even more he will be God's beloved son. Then God offers a chance for some extreme makeover to these three frightened disciples who six days earlier did not know if they wanted to make the cut. God says, after acknowledging that the shinning, radiant, changed figure before them is the chosen one, "listen to him!"

The disciples are given the chance to receive the needed extreme make over that it is going to take to follow Jesus to Jerusalem and a waiting cross. It is the same extreme makeover we are offered today.

In Rachel Remen's wonderful book, "My Grandfather's Blessing" she tells of her grandfather, who was a respected Rabbi, putting his aged hands on her seven year old head and giving her the pet name, *Neshumele*. She writes:

He would rest his hands lightly on the top of my head and begin by thanking God for me and for making him my grandpa. He would specifically mention my struggles during that week and tell God something about me that was true . . . Then he would give me his blessing and ask the long ago women I knew from many stories—Sarah, Rachael, Rebekah, and Lean—to watch over me . . .

(My family seemed to always want more of me . . . to do better in school) But my grandfather did not care for such things. For him I was already enough. And somehow when I was with him I knew with absolute certainty that this was so. My grandfather looked at me as no one else had and called me by my special name, *Neshume-le*, which means 'beloved little soul.'[1]

On the mount of Transfiguration the Jesus of history receives the divine makeover. He is acknowledged by the God of the universe and his heavenly father as the one we have been waiting for. The disciples are then given their own divine makeover by this one who has been transfigured before them.

Jesus reaches over and, like Rachel's beloved grandfather, Jesus touches them and says, "Get up and do not be afraid." Jesus is blessed and transformed by his father and he immediately offers a blessing to those who seek to follow him.

It is the same for us today. If we dare to follow this beloved Son of God we must hear the transforming words of blessing from the God of Jesus. Are you aware that you, too, are a *Neshume-le*? You are a "beloved little soul" to God.

We must first know this if we are going to come down off the mountain of transformation and follow this Jesus through the journey of Lent. If there is any season of the Christian year where we are offered the chance for some extreme makeover it is this season of Lent. Lent is a time of repentance, confession, and renewal. It is the season of letting go in order to have more. It is a time of going down so we can come up.

None of this may make sense in the language of the world but this is God's offer for some extreme makeover. I read this week of a woman who became frustrated after a number of years because the rabbits would always eat the tender green shoots that came up from her bulbs that she had planted before winter.

---

1. Remen, *My Grandfather's Blessing*, 23.

Finally someone told her that all she needed to do was put a six-inch high fence around the bulbs. The rabbits could jump the fence if they desired but they would not because it was just enough of an obstacle to lead them toward some other green grasses nearby.

In Lent we put up some small fences so that we can have more. Some farmers were recently surprised when they learned that an effort called perm culture could help them be more efficient in their farming. Instead of letting their cattle roam freely over the entire land they were advised to fence off certain sections and keep the cattle within those sections. This would let certain other parts of the land rest.

Not only did this allow parts of the land rest the cattle fertilized a small portion of the land within the fence and the grasses grew even richer. Another added benefit was that the woman who lived on the farm and who loved to use the natural herbs that grew in the fields for her cooking discovered all sorts of new natural herbs that she had not been able to pick before. She wondered where these plants came from and then discovered that they had been in the soil all along but that they had been "trodden under foot by the relentless activity of the cows so they were never able to grow into their fullness."[2]

This is the chance we are given in the letting go and going down of Lent. We are given the chance for some extreme makeover whereby we can fence off some parts of our lives. Giving up certain things will allow other things to flourish. There are some things that may never be added to our lives unless we fence off some places and allow for some needed growth.

It all begins for Jesus in a moment of extreme makeover when he hears his father say, "This is my beloved." Can it begin for us today on the edge of a possible Lenten journey? Can we hear our father say, "*Neshume-le*. You are my beloved little soul."

Each Lent I am faced with some parts of my life that need some extreme makeover. Every Lent I am made aware of ways I cannot follow this Jesus who asks me to walk with him to the cross at Jerusalem. I cannot do it by myself. I cannot change without some changes and some makeover. I need some fences for some things to grow. The whole discipline of Lent, the letting go, the going down, is so that we can be changed and blessed in order that we might be a blessing for others.

2. Muller, *Sabbath*, 44.

Before we get to the hard part, before we ask for some extreme make-over, we need to hear the divine words of blessing, "You are *Neshume-le*. We are to God a beloved little soul." Jesus says again to us, "Do not be afraid, you are beloved. I have come to bless you before I take you off the mountain of change. I give you the chance to be new as you face my cross. It is not only me who is beloved of God. You too are . . .

Neshume-le"

APPENDIX SEVEN

Lent: Which Part is Yours?

LUKE 15:1–3, 11–32

A Sermon for Lent

OKAY TODAY IS SUNDAY at the *Improv*. What if I wonder through the congregation today and ask you to pick your part in the drama? Then I lure you up to the "stage" and give you a few props to help you act your part.

The story of the prodigal son supposedly is one of the most familiar stories in the bible. Even people who think Matthew, Mark, Luke, and John are the latest names claiming paternity rights to the Anna Nicole Smith baby, seem to know the story of the prodigal son who leaves home with his nest egg and loses everything on wine, women, and song only to return home with his tail between his legs and be lovingly received in the waiting arms of his father.

The problem with such a familiar story is that if we are not careful we will listen in a passive even lazy fashion. The story will be like elevator music that we somehow know the tune to but cannot quite remember the title. It's nice but it does not make much of an impact on us.

Well, not so today because I am asking you to pick your part in the drama and improvise on how you will act out the part. According to biblical scholarship the word "parable" means, "to cast along side of." A parable is a short story that is meant to ask you something. The basic question is, "How does this story compare to where you are or how you act?"

A parable is an invitation into the story in order to get you to see something in a different way or to allow you a change of environment so that you can make a judgment about something. So today you do not get to buy your ticket and watch the play. I invite you to take your "prop" and find yourself in the living of the story.

Here are your props for your *improv*. In chair number 1 we have the props for the prodigal. Here is a party hat. The prodigal is in the unreachable stage of his life. He loses perspective and is self-absorbed. His father evidently knows this because he allows the young rebel to take his trust fund that is to be used only after the father's death and run away to God knows where.

The son is saying basically, "I wish you were dead. Who are you to tell me what to do? I want my freedom and I want it now . . . and I want the resources to do whatever the heck I want." How many parents have heard this message from children who think they are grown up and who want us out of the picture? I call this the unreachable stage. As a parent you reach for your flesh and blood and they pull away from you like you are some kind of alien. They reject you and make you feel like you might as well drop dead.

The word in the story for what happens to and with the prodigal is *asotos*. It is translated "riotous living." It is a derivative of the word used in the New Testament for "to save" someone, *sozo*. In other words the prodigal is so unreachable that he is beyond the power of saving.

He ends up in the pigpen with nothing. In the original text it does not say what you heard this morning. The translation is that, "no one gave him anything." The actual language says, "that no one gave to him."[1] In other words no one gives him understanding, the time of day, or any form of love. He ends up "without."

Anybody here ever been there or played that part? In AA they call this concept praying for a high bottom. People in the 12 step programs know that the only way they will ever really learn anything about changing destructive patterns is to "hit the bottom." If that is the case then the only thing to do is to pray that you have a "high bottom" so that you will hit it quick.

The prodigal does not have a high bottom. He loses everything. He is "without." He does not realize what I tried to make my rebellious children at least see. They are playing in wet cement. Their mistakes of youth, although somewhat understandable and even allowable, are going to make

---

1. Long, *Textweek Online*.

footprints that will dry and when they come to their senses later the imprints will have dried and they will have to deal with the consequences.

The prodigal plays in the wet cement and the cost is the loss of his resources, probably his health, and he thinks the love and respect of his family and friends. So he limps home barefoot knowing that he will not even receive from his father the sandals (hold up sandals as the second prop for the prodigal) that are fit for a member of the house. He will remain barefoot like a slave in his father's household but at least he will have shelter and something to eat.

Chair number 2 contains the props for the father. Here we have not sandals but running shoes. And here are binoculars. Not only is the father constantly looking down the road each evening hoping to see the silhouette of his lost child he even has his running shoes on so that he can run toward him to embrace him if he shows up.

This is a scandal of the highest degree in the Eastern culture in which Jesus tells the story. For an older man to run means that he must lift his tunic thus exposing his legs. You say, "no big deal." No, this is a very big deal. This is a sign of loss of dignity. An older man never runs especially to a child who has screamed to all those around, "I wish my father was dead."

In Jesus' culture to do this would be to say to the whole social fabric of the surrounding village, "I cast aside the norms and customs and rules of parenting." The other parents would say something like, "His running toward his wayward child means that it is okay to sass parents and break rules. This is the undoing of our culture."

The old man cares not. He puts down his binoculars that afternoon that he sees his child and runs to embrace him. It is a love and grace that is beyond imagining.

I remember the night I looked out the window at 2 o'clock in the morning and whispered a prayer to God:

> I do not care that I am a minister and that what my daughter is doing is an embarrassment to me as a parent and a role model. Please God just let her come home alive. I put off my values I long for her to have because she has rejected those. I will leave them beside the road. Just let me see some headlights come down the driveway so that I will know that I still have her body if I cannot have her soul. Just give me a chance.

Henry Nouwen wrote a book about the prodigal and he uses Rembrandt's painting that depicts an old man with his hands on the back of a kneeling prodigal son who leans into the old man's robes. Nouwen says that if you look close you can see that Rembrandt actually has the father's hands as two different style hands. One hand seems firm and gripping. It is the tired hand of the father, but the other hand is open and flexible. It is the hurting and nurturing hand of the mother.[2]

On chair number three rests the props for the elder brother. Since we have used shoes for the other characters here are the shoes for the elder brother. They are combat boots. They are rigid and ready for work.

When the elder brother rejects his father's plea to come to the party being held for the lost child the elder brother uses the word *douleuo*, which is translated "to slave over." The elder brother has slaved in his father's house. Everything is duty. He is the son who slaves over his religion, his studies, and his relationships. His anger robs him of any love. He is locked in his goodness.

Here is his other prop a yardstick. He spends his life measuring everything and everyone, judging whether or not they "measure up" to the standard he sets. His anger leads to such a righteous indignation that when his measuring words are cast toward his wild brother who returns he says, "Here I stayed home slaving away in your service and that son of yours spends his money on prostitutes and such."

Of course there is no mention of prostitutes but the combat boot, yard stick holding, locked up tight older brother is projecting his own dark side onto his wicked brother. The elder brother screams disrespectfully into the face of his father and announces, "I have been good. I have been good," but even in his words are the longing he has to be bad for a while. The darkness is within each of us and it often hides behind the combat boots of being good.

The father looks into the rigid stare of his other lost son standing solid in his boots and says, *teknon* which is not "son" but "My child . . . everything I have is yours." The older boy kicks up the dust so that it covers his dad's running shoes and throws down his yardstick at his father's feet. "That son of yours is no brother of mine. Party till you drop if you want. I'll have none of it and none of you or him," and he walks away.

---

2. Nouwen, *The Return of the Prodigal*, 99.

Here are the props. Here are the parts for you to play. I want to tell you I have played all the parts at one time or another in my life.

I have strayed like the prodigal. I have wanted too much too quick. I have found my own far country.

I have waited by the window with my running shoes on and watched with my emotional binoculars. I have put love above rules.

And I have been that religious moralistic elder brother judging those other people who are not like me. I use them to make me feel more secure and more "in." I have silently screamed that it is not fair that some people seem to get away with things that they should not when they ought to get what they deserve. I have my notched yardstick.

I see our nation sometimes playing these parts. We can be lost like prodigal. We can be a loving forgiving nation, or we can and it seems often are like the elder child unwilling to see how locked in we are to old ways and unwilling to change and risk learning from mistaken judgment.

Here are the props and the "parts." I suppose again today there is one who watches as we act out our parts. The hands of our God reflect both the hands of the father and the mother. Our God is the one who understands all the roles but according to the one who first tells the story, the chair that holds the props for God, is chair number two.

So for all of us parents who know the wounded love of parenting, and especially for the elder brother/sister and prodigal son/daughter parts of us, I offer you a God of the running shoes who loves you and me beyond measure. And I remind you of a God of the binoculars who is always looking for us to come home.

Christ the King Sunday: The Kingdom of God

A Strange Democracy

"Christ the King Sunday"

LUKE 23:33–34

WHEN YOU THINK OF a king what comes to mind. This time of year when the "Wizard of Oz" is often replayed on TV, I remember that timid lion who so longed to have courage. The "cowardly lion" knows that as a lion he is supposed to rule the forest, but he does not know if he has what it takes to be king of the forest. He longs to be such as he sings,

> If I were king of the forest,
> Not Queen, not Duke, not Price,
> My regal robes of the forest
> Would be satin, not cotton, not chintz.
> I'd command each thing, be it fish or fowl,
> With a woof and a woof, and a royal growl.
> As I'd click my heel
> The trees would kneel,
> And the mountains bow,
> And the bulls kowtow,
> And the sparrow would take wing,
> If I were King.[1]

1. Arlen, "If I Were King of the Forrest." Wizard of Oz Soundtrack. MGM, 1996.

I had a football coach in high school who liked to think he was a king and who ruled with an iron fist. One of his favorite expressions was, "Let's get something straight. This team is not a democracy. You don't get a vote. I'm in charge."

When I get a little too high on my high horse and start suggesting that things should go my way, my wife uses an old expression, "Who died and made you king?" This is a reminder that I am not her football coach and that she gets a vote.

You will hear me talk a lot about equality and justice because those who seek to be followers of Christ must recognize that we are all one family in the kingdom of God. The truth is that today we come to a stop sign on the road. It is time to acknowledge that this kingdom of God is a strange democracy. This democracy has a king.

I know democracies are not supposed to have kings. Well, I told you it is a strange democracy. Abraham Lincoln once said, "As I would not be a slave so I would not be a master. This expresses my idea of democracy." Reinhold Niebuhr once stated, "Man's capacity for justice makes democracy possible but man's inclination to injustice makes democracy necessary."

The kingdom that Jesus offers his followers has elements of a need for democracy in that no person is called to be master over another and the only servant hood required is that we serve each other. Our inclination toward selfishness and injustice also makes democracy in this kingdom necessary.

But in the case of the kingdom of God the answer to the question, "Who died and made you king?" is found in the shadow of a cross. Today is the day we stop and realize that our leader's death makes him our king. This democracy needs a king.

Because of our inclination to make our own little kingdoms or our desire to rule the kingdom our way, we need leadership. It seems that if we do not have such servant hood leadership that is offered by Jesus we make the kingdom of God into our kind of club or we put certain things up to a kind of vote and overrule certain concepts that are essential to the kingdom.

In other words what today is really about is the answer to the question, "Who and what rules our lives?" We get a say in this strange kingdom but we do not get to rule. That is not so popular these days, especially in an America where the divine right of kings went the way of the dinosaurs. In our need for rampant individuality and our desire for self-fulfillment we say to Jesus by our actions, "Who died and made you king?"

Part of our problem is that not only do we have a strange kingdom, we have a strange king. In the game of chess the match is over when you lose your king. You can lose your queen, your knight, and even your castle; but when you lose your king the game is over. On God's game board the victory is won by the king loosing. What kind of rules are these?

It seems we have a king who rules by example. His example comes from a kingly dictate when he says, "I have come not to be served but to serve." His kingdom has subjects that are to do as he did when he knelt and washed his subjects feet. Risk, forgiveness, spending time with outcasts, and being willing to lose for the kingdom are all elements of his rule.

We cannot dress up our king and make him something he is not. There is the story of a man who was destined to be king of his land. Before assuming his crown he decided to visit his people dressed as a beggar. Most people had nothing to do with him.

After being crowned he again visited one of his wealthy subjects who of course invited in the king and offered him a fine meal. As they sat at the table the king began to take the sumptuous food and spread it over his fine clothes. The wealthy host was appalled but since this was the king he refrained from comment.

After watching the king continue mashing the food into his robe and silk shirt the host could stand it not longer. "What are you doing sire," asked the host? "Well," said the king, "I came to visit you last year dressed as a beggar and you turned me away. The only thing different about me is my clothes so I assumed that you wanted to feed my clothes."

Jesus comes as a servant. We cannot dress up what he asks of us. He is crucified between two outcasts. One tries to dress up what Jesus is and says, "Can't you be another kind of king and get us out of this mess?" The other thief simply acknowledges Jesus' kingship and asks to be remembered when Jesus receives his real crown. Today which thief is remembered? It is the one who gains entrance to paradise by letting go with Jesus in his loosing.

Our king once said that the kingdom of God is like a fishing net. The word he uses is not the word for a small net but is rather the Greek word *sagene* which is translated seine or dragnet. It is the kind of net that is often outlawed in fishing today because it is drug along the bottom of the water and collects all kinds of fish rather than the specific fish for which one is licensed to catch. Such nets for instance catch dolphins when tuna is the catch of the day.

Jesus kingdom is like a dragnet. All sorts of people are going to come up with you if this net catches you. There will be people in the net whom you do not want to be with. There will be conservatives, liberals, bible thumpers, and heretics. There will be people who support the need for war and people who think it is immoral. There will be straight people and gay people, Democrats who are sad and Republicans who are rejoicing. According to bumper sticker theology when it comes to casting the Christian "net" the saying from the mouth of Jesus is, "You catch'em and I'll clean'em." Jesus is after all crucified as king between two outcasts who are drug up.

Our king is one who bends down and washes feet. He teaches us to share our gifts. He rules by offering himself and he wins by loosing, but he is king of this strange democracy. He died and God made him king. In God's kingdom we cannot rule ourselves. We make terrible masters. History proves that. In God's democracy we are to be servants who risk losing to find.

In my life I am reminded that the word "ego" can stand for "edging God out." I need a king to remind me that my ego cannot be enthroned to rule my life. I need a king who is the King of Kings and Lord of Lords. Today I kneel before Christ the King.

(At this time I kneel before a chair placed in front of the altar. Behind the chair is placed the processional cross on which is hung a crown of thorns. Beside the chair I pour some water into a bowl and place a towel beside the bowl. Beside the chair is placed a shepherd's staff. "Jesus Remember Me" is played after which I pray the following:)

Jesus I need a king. I cannot rule my own life. I make a terrible master. Today I acknowledge you as King of Kings and Lord of Lords. Teach me your ways of service. Show me how to kneel. Teach me how to fish. Catch me in your net. Shepherd me when I get lost. From your cross remind me that even in losing there is victory. O King who died for me, help me to live for you. Amen.

Appendix Nine

Pentecost Sunday: Passionate Kisses
or a Lukewarm Handshake

ACTS 2:1–6, 14–17 / JOHN 14:15–17, 25–26

WHEN ASKED IF A certain young man was not getting his work done because maybe he was "burned out," his supervisor responded, "There's no way he could be burned out because he never caught fire." Today is Pentecost day, the day a bunch of people who claimed to be followers of Jesus caught fire.

These men were floundering a bit not knowing what to do after Jesus had left them. They were told to wait so they were waiting for the future. John Richardson said that when it comes to the future there are three kinds of people: those who make it happen, those who let it happen, and those who wonder what happened.[1]

These bewildered disciples on Pentecost day were a little bit of all three. They had "let it happen" when Jesus was with them. They seemed not to be able to stem the tide of events. Jesus had laid it on the line in Jerusalem, gotten himself crucified much to the disappointment of those who wanted him to be king of the heap, and then suddenly came back from the grave and turned everything upside down, including "death."

The disciples were left to wonder "what happened" and what did it all mean. They were still wondering what they were supposed to do when the shutters flew open and wind of the Spirit blew their plans all over the floor while flames danced over their heads. It was evidently time to

1. Nanus, *Visionary Leadership*, 133.

163

"make" the future happen and now they were equipped with a burning presence called the Holy Spirit to help them "make it happen."

Today on this birthday of the church are we who are the faith descendents of these first spirit filled disciples more like passionate kisses or are we more like a lukewarm handshake? Mary Chapin Carpenter sings in her song, "Passionate Kisses,"

> Is it too much to ask
>   I want a comfortable bed that won't hurt my back,
> Food to fill me up, and warm clothes and all that stuff
> Shouldn't I have this, shouldn't I have this
> Shouldn't I have all of this and,
> Passionate kisses, passionate kisses, passionate kisses from you
> Do I want too much am I going overboard to want that touch?[2]

It is interesting that the United Methodist church's latest theme to tell the world who we really are is called "Igniting Ministries." Our United Methodist logo is the cross and the flame, but can we be igniting if we are not on fire? Are we really passionate about our faith or is our faith more like the handshake I gave a man after I preached my first sermon as a student.

I put my hand into his and softly shook his hand. The man squeezed my hand so that I felt a bit of pain and he said, "My God son, with a handshake like that you will never be a preacher. Put something into it like you mean it." I still do not know if he was referring only to my lukewarm handshake or my sermon, but I still remember what he said.

This man was looking for passion and I had given him a mild response.

Is there no danger of us burning out in our faith because we never caught the Pentecost fire? Our founder John Wesley was accused by the church of his day of being too "enthusiastic." Wesley was guarded about lowering himself to go preach outdoors. It was not the custom of his Anglican heritage. He had been cautioned about the raw nature of taking holy things outside, but Wesley took the burning message to the people and that is the reason we have a Methodist church.

Wesley once said of his preaching, "God has set me on fire and the people come and watch me burn." So today we have at least two reasons to burn with passion about our faith. We have the original story of that kin-

---

2. Carpenter, *Passionate Kisses.*" Come On, Come On. Sony, 1992.

dling fire of Pentecost at which a bunch of "wondering what happened" disciples" went out and changed the world. We also have a founder of the Methodist movement who with burning enthusiasm singed 18th century England.

Maybe we ought to honestly ask what it is that gets us all fired up? Sports can do it for some of us. I am amazed as I walk through the underpass when I get to go to some of those Carolina Panthers home games. People scream as loud as they can just to hear their voices echo within the walls of the bridge as they walk to the gladiatorial game. These people can be accused of being "too enthusiastic."

When is the last time you were accused of being too enthusiastic about your faith? Or is there no danger of you burning out because there is no fire?

Well hang on because today is igniting day. This is a chance to ask God to light our fire so that our faith can be more like passionate kisses than a lukewarm handshake.

Jesus is leaving his disciples but he tells them in our story today that they will receive power to be like him. He tries to tell them that they already possess most of what it takes to create a new way of life but they will still need some wind to make the ship sail. In other words God plants a purpose within those who will listen and all that is needed is power to go with the purpose.

Rick Warren's bestselling book, "The Purpose Driven Life" is so popular because this is really what it is saying. The book begins with the question that both believers and nonbelievers ask, "Why am I here?" Warren's book offers the reasons. He says we are here because God wanted us here. We are here to realize that we are part of a family of God and that we are not to go it alone. We are here to be formed into the likeness not of the world but of Christ. We are here to learn to serve not to learn to be served. And we are here to discover our mission or purpose, and everyone has a purpose.[3]

So in other words to use Warren's vision to help us see what we are to do to make the future happen we would ask God for the gift of the power of a spirit beyond ourselves to help us really be ourselves. When we discover our purpose that purpose will have elements of being part of the family of God, being formed by the spirit of Christ, and being in

3. Warren, *The Purpose Driven Life*, 7–8.

service to God's people rather than constantly seeking to possess and gain for ourselves.

You may have heard of the research being done on the Gospel of Thomas. This writing is believed to have been composed about the same time as the Gospel of John. It was recently discovered in Egypt. While scholars are not ready to admit it to the New Testament because of some of its non-orthodox statements some believe that within this writing, which contains only sayings of Jesus, that we may have some authentic words of Jesus.

In the Gospel of Thomas Jesus says, "If you bring forth that which is within in, what you bring forth will save you. If you do not bring forth what is within you, what you do not bring forth will destroy you."[4] Jesus also says, "When you come to know yourselves, then you will be known, and you will see that it is you who are the children of the living father . . . fail to know this and you dwell in poverty."[5]

Whether this gospel should be part of our understanding of Jesus or not these words do continue what Jesus is saying to his disciples in John. Jesus tells them that the Kingdom is within them and that God's purpose is planted like seeds waiting to sprout forth. What is needed is to know what is inside you and then call upon the passionate power of the Spirit of God to make it happen.

So on this day of power receiving which brought forth the birth of the Christian church in which we now sit I ask you and me, "What is our purpose and where is our passion and power?"

We are not created by God to simply let things happen or end up wondering what happened. Christians have a purpose to stand against the powers of darkness, hate, bigotry, and discrimination of all kinds. We are ones called not to comply with a world whose mantra is security at all costs, gain at any expense, and if you are not like me you are not in. Disciples of Jesus are living a purpose that involves Christ-like service.

God wants you to know who you are for there is a God seed in you. One of the things I always want a church to do is help individuals discover the divinity within them. Then the church is to help people share that divinity . . . with passion.

---

4. Paterson, Stephen, et al. *The Gospel of Thomas*, 3b.

5. Ibid., 70.

Today I want you to think of your purpose in life for a moment. I cannot tell you what it is but if it is to conform to the Christian way it will involve being part of the family of God, knowing that you are God's child, and giving to the world in service and mission for you know you owe life something.

Today I want to emphasis the passion and power that is available to us for living out our purpose. We can be ignited so that we are set on fire for living God's purpose. The Spirit of God is the power beyond us. The Spirit of God is fire and wind.

"Spirit" in Hebrew is *rhuah* which means wind, or breath. When some doctor slapped your hind end that first day of your new life, you gasped for breath. You celebrate it now as your birthday. What is your Spirit birthday? Is there a moment you can remember when God's empowering wind filled you? We all need some breath of God, some spirit to empower our purpose.

Sometimes the Spirit is gentle like the breeze and that is refreshing news, but for some of us there is a need for the shutters of lives to be blown open by this same "wind" because we are living for ourselves only. Today is "Spirit Day" in the Christian church. Ask for the breath. Ask for the wind. Ask for the fire. We need to offer this world discipleship that resembles passionate kisses rather than lukewarm handshakes.

Appendix Ten

Be Still and Know

1 KINGS 19:1-15 / PSALM 46

MANY OF US HAVE a hard time with being still and keeping silent. This reminds me of Earl and Diane who were married for many years and who always went to the county fair each year. Every year Earl would say, "Diane I want to ride in the stunt plane this year" Each year they would pass the section where the stunt plane pilot would be sitting and Earl would say "Come on let's ride."

Every year Diane would say, "You know that is too dangerous." She would then lecture him about the senselessness of such an endeavor and she would always end her lecture with a talk about money." "But it is only $50," Earl would reply. Diane would say, "After all Earl $50 is $50." "But I'm 75 years old Diane and I have been wanting to do this for years." "$50 is $50 Earl."

Finally the stunt plane pilot after hearing this same argument for years at the fair said to the both of them as they stood in front of his plane, "I'll make you a deal. I'll take you up for a ride. If you will not say a word for the whole ride I will not charge you anything. But if either of you say one word it will be $50."

They looked at each other and decided it was a good deal so they climbed in the open-air cockpit of the stunt plane just behind the pilot. The pilot did his usual loop de loops and death spirals but not a word came from Earl and Diane. He was surprised so he added some extra turns and loops. Still not a word came from the couple.

He landed the plane and as the engine came to a stop he turned slightly and said to them, "Well I must admit I am surprised you did not say a word." Earl leaned forward and said, "Well it was hard especially

168

when Diane fell out of the plane on one of those first loops but you know $50 is $50."

Being still and silent is a challenge for many of us including me. Since we are so involved in doing we often equate being still and being silent with doing nothing.

My old friend Lester had a farm to which he often invited groups of people for picnics. He always told the children who were there the same story of the old miner who was buried on the property. He said that the legend has it that the old miner found gold but he died with his secret and no one knew where the gold was on the property.

Then Lester would say, "But if you get real close to his grave the legend says that he will speak to you in a whisper from his grave." And then Lester would smile and say, "Lean down and an you can hear the old miner whisper from his grave, 'Nothing at all, nothing at all.'" He would then laugh as he looked into the surprised faces of the children to whom he offered the riddle.

Do we think that when we get silent and still that we are "doing" nothing at all? Today our scriptures lead us to an understanding that there is power and knowledge in the silence and the stillness. Elijah is a man's man. The story we hear today follows an event at which Elijah slays 800 of the Baal prophets and calls down fire from heaven. He wins the "Super Bowl" of religious battles. Elijah is a doer and relishes proclaiming a God of power and might.

But when the going gets tough he does not quite know what to do. Jezebel puts out a contract on him and finds whatever it is that pulls Elijah's strings. Elijah panics and finds that he has nowhere to hide. He tries to hide in the wilderness and since he is experiencing religious burn out he even tries to hide from the God whose work he is supposed to be doing. God provides sustenance for him even in his hiding. Finally Elijah sneaks into a cave but God pursues him and tells him to stand at the entrance of the cave.

This man of God who is accustomed to using and proclaiming God's power then witnesses a show of sorts. The usual places that Elijah expects God to show up in obvious ways do not benefit Elijah this time. There is earthquake, wind, and fire but God is not in the earthquake, wind, and fire.

Elijah thinks he needs another powerful event in order to know God but this time the knowing does not come in a billboard or in a majestic miracle. This time Elijah is offered a different way of knowing. God is in the "still small voice" or in the literal translation God is within "the sound of sheer stillness."

This is often counter to our Western, doing oriented mind that makes the spiritual pilgrimage into a kind of project to do. Our conscious minds whisper to us that to be still is to "do nothing at all." But here is where the spiritual journey is counter cultural. Psalm 46 offers us another way of knowing, "Be still and *know* that I am God."

We are spiritual beings that act like we are not. We so often act as if there is only one level to our awareness and that it the level of the ego that must get things accomplished. The ego consciousness says over and over to itself and others, "I must prove myself by doing."

God makes us with the ability to go below this level of consciousness because below our ego, which is often called in spiritual language the false self, there is the essence of who we are. This is not some New Age strange esoteric kind of thing. This is for all of us. Elijah finds it out just after the earthquake of activity ceased, and the wind of busy schedules subsides, and the fire of the rat race seems to be extinguished by an ever-slight breeze.

Here is the way one writer puts it:

> But spiritual awareness is actually a way of perceiving, just as ordinary awareness is a way of perceiving. And as with ordinary awareness, there is a sense of identity or selfhood generated through this mode of perception. The big difference between them is that whereas ordinary awareness perceives through self-reflexive consciousness, which splits the world into subject and object; spiritual awareness perceives through an intuitive grasp of the whole and an innate sense of belonging. It's something like sounding the note G on the piano and instantly hearing the D and the B that surround it and make it a chord. And since spiritual awareness is perception based on harmony, the sense of selfhood arising out of it is not plagued by that sense of isolation and anxiety that dominates life at the ordinary level of awareness.[1]

There is a way of knowing that is constantly available to us but we are occupied with the search for the earthquake, wind, and fire so we miss the knowing in the stillness. Within us is the place of God. We are not machines or computers that are programmed. Life is not simply a matter of booting up each morning and running the software.

1. Bourgeault, "Silence is God's First Language," *Beliefnet.*

God plants within each person the place of "indwelling." How often do we go there? How often do we pass by this place as if it is only for those saints of God that we read about in books? This place is for you and me but we must let go of a bit of ordinary consciousness in order to get to this place of knowing where we often think we will hear "nothing at all."

It is in this "nothing" that we come to know something that we will never "know" in the doing. It is often in this "place" where God can do with us what God can never do in our scattered, busy lives of constant activity.

Quantum Physics even helps us understand this reality. Within quantum physics there is the perceived principal call the "non local" understanding of matter. This principal states that particles and events that appear to be separate from one another in space and time maintain a connection or correlation with one another.

This means that pairs of photons that are sent off at the speed of light from each other retain a connection even after traveling many kilometers, whereby a change in the polarity of one proton causes a corresponding change in the other. This non-local understanding of matter means that two seemingly separate things are connected despite an apparent distance between the two.

You and I are made of particles that come from an origin of light. That origin is God. Do you feel separate from God? Does the distance between your mortality and the divine seem great and expansive? We so often look to the large, the powerful, the earthquake, wind and fire of life and we fail to be still and look inward. There we will discover the indwelling of the One who created us to be light. We are always connected but we fail to "know" this.

Another principal in quantum physics helps us understand this scattered reality. It seems that a laser that is not focused properly means that its power is unavailable because the particles of light are diffuse. But with an effect called stimulated emission an infinitesimal amount of light from a highly coherent laser can bring order to the chaotic atoms of the (ineffective) laser. The power of the coherent laser purifies and transforms the disharmonious, ineffective laser, rendering it highly coherent and powerful enough to become a potentiating laser itself.

Anybody here ever feel scattered? If this works in quantum physics, then surly it can "work" on the particles of the very soul that God creates in the first place. Be still and know. Be still and allow the scattered particles of our lives to be realigned so that we might experience the power of what seems like "nothing at all."

Annie Dillard tells a story in her book, "Pilgrim at Tinker Creek" of the day she comes around a building just in time to see a Mockingbird dive toward the earth with the sun in the background of its descent. Just at the last moment the bird spreads its wings and gently steps onto the grass. The beauty of the moment is mystical but she ponders the thought similar to the idea that if a tree falls in the forest and no one is there to hear it is there any sound?

Dillard writes, "If I had not come around that building at precisely that moment and seen it would there have been grace and beauty there?" She goes on to say that grace is always there but we so often hurry by our buildings on the way to someplace else. She closes by writing, "The least we can do is try to be there."[2]

Elijah discovers that he must step aside from the earthquake, wind, and fire and "be there." When he is "there" he discovers God in the stillness.

St. John of the Cross says that "silence is God's first language." I discovered this in the midst of a very painful time in my life when I felt distant from God. I did an Elijah kind of thing and went off to hide from my congregation. The church I was serving was a small rural church and I was not doing well and felt that I was being ineffective. If I was "God's man" I was not going over very well. My words seemed to be falling on deaf ears and I was becoming dry and bitter.

The leader of the event to which I went to "hide" asked us to observe a day of silence the first day. I was mad. I needed to talk, to spill my guts. I needed some instruction, some advice. I needed to "do" something.

I did not need to do "nothing at all" like being silent. I grabbed a book and charged up a nearby mountain to get away from everybody. I did not find a cave but I did stop for a moment beside a huge bolder. Then it happened. A shadow came over me. I looked around and there it was again. Then I looked up and saw the cause of the shadow.

A large bird was at just the right angle to be circling in a pattern that brought it between the sun's light and my path. The shadow came from above. As I looked up I noticed that the bird was soaring higher and higher in the wind. But do you know what it was doing in order to go

---

2. Dillard, *Pilgrim at Tinker Creek*, 8.

higher and higher? It was doing "nothing at all." It was simply spreading its wings and allowing the wind currents to lift it.

I leaned against the boulder and starting to cry. "What the heck is the matter with me?" I wondered. "Why am I so affected by the shadow of a bird soaring on the wind?" Then there came the breeze, the few particles of the same breeze that lifted the wings of the bird. And the breeze whispered to me, "Jody, quit flapping your wings."

In that moment when I witnessed a bird do nothing to gain its power I discovered for myself Elijah's lesson. Be still and know. . . .

Appendix Eleven

Careful . . . There Really Is a Dark Side

JAMES 3:3—4:8

THERE WAS THIS VERY religious woman who lived beside a self-proclaimed atheist. The atheist was always giving the woman a hard time about her belief in God. One day the atheist overheard the woman praying to God for some groceries because she was low on money and could not buy what she needed.

The atheist knew exactly what to do. He went to the grocery store, bought a big bag of food, placed it on the woman's doorstep, and rang the doorbell. He then ran behind some bushes. When the woman came to the door she fell down on her knees and started thanking God for the groceries.

The atheist jumped from behind the bushes and shouted, "Ah ha, there is no God. I bought the groceries. No God sent them to you." Upon hearing this the woman raised her hands and starting praising God even more.

"What the heck are you doing? I told you the food came from me not from God." The woman rose to her feet, smiled at her neighbor, and said, "I knew that God would send me some groceries but I didn't know that he was going to make the devil pay for them."

The truth in this story is not that there is in fact a devil but that the devil is your neighbor. In fact the devil is always close by.

A debate is still going on as to whether there really is a personal devil or is the figure of a devil the personification of the presence of evil. The answer is, "yes." If you need today to believe in a personal figure called the devil in order to allow for the very real power of evil in this world then go on believing. If you do not believe there is a figure called the devil be very careful. The devil is your neighbor or at least the lure and power of the dark side is very close by . . . always.

There are only 3 references to Satan in the whole Old Testament. Part of the reason for this is the need to maintain the oneness of God in the presence of so many different religions that believed in all kinds of gods. As Hebrew monotheism encountered Persian thought something called Zoroasterism, a kind of dualism, was created as a way to figure out why a good God could allow for evil in the world. Zoroasterism believed in two dueling gods. One was good and one was evil. The duel between the good god and the bad god created the world.

Hebrew thought could not quite allow for there to be another God so just before New Testament times a number of writings tried to explain "the dark side of life." Combining extra-biblical material and a few references from the Hebrew bible the story of a battle in heaven between good angels and rebellious angels was put together.

Lucifer, which means "light-bearer," was cast out of heaven and thrown down to earth with his army of rebellious angels. The original story seems to be best told in a book not in our bible called, "The Book of Secrets of Enoch." Lucifer is also known as Beelzebub, or Lord of Flies.

By the time of Jesus a full-fledged belief in demons and angels was prevalent. Jesus used language about the devil and his angels. Scholars argue over the issue of did Jesus really believe in demons or did he just use the language of the people so that they could understand his power over evil forces. Here again the answer seems to be, "yes."

We have no way of knowing just what Jesus really believed in his own mind. What we do know is that he took the presence of evil very seriously and so should we.

Walter Wink and others point to the reality that the world-view of the New Testament was one where spirits filled the air. The New Testament calls the devil a roaring lion, a dragon, a serpent, the ruler of this world, the enemy, and the evil one. Jesus used devil language either because he believed it literally or at least to make his point that we who wish to follow him better pay attention to the "dark side."

What has happened is that with the Enlightenment and the ensuing scientific world-view the transcendent has collapsed. Many people no longer see the world as a heaven up there and a hell down there with demons and angels running around. Heaven has faded as uncountable galaxies have been discovered. Hell is absorbed in the fields of depth psychology that relegates sin to old fashioned and outdated thinking and comes up with the language of dysfunction and imbalance.

What we see in our own day is a reaction to this by very conservative or fundamentalist religious people who are again using ancient devil language to describe what they see as spiritual warfare. The problem is that this language is being used to both scare and demonize whoever the opposition might be. So in America now we are fighting a war on terrorism with an enemy who is obviously evil while at the same time that enemy is calling us "the great Satan."

Here is the truth. We need to be careful who we call the enemy and Satan because the devil actually lives next door. Well, let's be even more honest, the dark side is even closer than next door. The dark side is always available to us within our own soul and self.

Of course the language of "the dark side" has been made famous and popular by the Star Wars movies. In these movies there is the ever-present "Force," which is the unifying principal that both causes and sustains all of life. There is the good side of the force and the dark side of the force.

The "Jedi" represent the light side of the force. Have you ever heard the code of the Jedi? Here it is:

> There is no emotion; there is peace
> There is no ignorance; there is knowledge
> There is no passion; there is serenity
> (There is no chaos; there is harmony)—sometimes not included
> There is no death; there is the Force

The champions of the dark side are called "the Sith." By the way Sith is the ancient Egyptian god of chaos, war, and storms. Here is the Sith Code:

> Peace is a lie; there is only passion
> Through passion, I gain strength
> Through strength, I gain power
> Through power, I gain victory
> Through victory, my chains are broken
> The Force shall set me free.

In this modern day mythology Anakin Skywalker succumbs to the Dark Side not because some devil makes him do it. This very powerful Jedi knight gives himself over to the powers of darkness because of his passion to gain power over life and even death. One outside himself lures

Anakin to the dark powers within his own soul but it is Anakin who decides to give himself over to the Dark Side.

Alexander Solzhenitsyn, living with the power of the communist state in Russia but knowing that demonizing the state and blaming it as the source of all evil was not the answer wrote the following:

> If only it were all so simple. If only there were evil people people somewhere insidiously committing evil deeds and it were necessary only to separate them from the rest of us and destroy them. But the dividing line between good and evil cuts through the heart of every human being, and who is willing to destroy a piece of his own heart?

There is evil in this world and God is in a battle with it. Our story clearly says that God will win the "war" but the last book of the bible, the Book of Revelation says that at times God's people will lose some of the battles. On this side of heaven we are still choosing between good and evil.

Lance Morrow, in his book "Evil: An Investigation," writes of how those who feel victimized often justify what is known as necessary evil. Hitler used this victimization to justify great wrongs done to Jews and others. The Serbs excused the horrors done to the Muslims because of the way they had been wronged years earlier. "Never forget" becomes the mantra for "necessary evil."[1]

In the aftermath of September 11 we must be careful of uttering the words, "never forget." Evil blinds us into thinking that the law of retribution is necessary. It is dangerous territory.

We must be careful, especially in the midst of something we call "a war on terror" to not demonize our enemy so much that we fall to see the darkness within our own selves and in our own nation. Jesus was very clear about this when he said that evil begins within one's own "eye." For Jesus the eye was the window of the soul and that is why he said, "Get the plank out of your own eye before you talk about the splinter in your neighbors eye." To think that the devil only lives next door is to fail to realize that the devil and the power of the dark side is as close as our own choices.

Evil can be woven into systems that use idealism to mask the truth. So it is true as I understand it that there is evil in some followers of Islam

---

1. Morrow, *Evil An Investigation*, 63.

as they interpret their sacred text in such a way as to distort it's intent because of their own bent, selfish, and idolatrous purposes.

But we must be careful as we critique other systems not to overlook the capacity for our own faith and political systems to become an idol that is used for selfish gain so that people are left in the shadows of indifference, poverty, and ignorance. I met with the Superintendent of Public Schools this week and listened to stories of our own school system where the need to combat seeds of evil are very present.

Lack of parental support, gangs becoming more prominent, and affluent parents like me turning away and looking only to my children's needs are part of the selfishness that is nurtured by the subtlety of the dark side of who I am. Most of the individuals in prison can link their deeds of darkness to lack of education and lack of nurture when they were young.

There is a scary passage in the book of Revelation when people confront evil in the form of "the Beast." The response is "woe is the Beast who can stand against it." Great evil is done when good people do nothing. Poverty and poor education in our own land is condoned by the Dark Side, which says, "It's okay to take care of only those whom you love." That does not sound like evil does it?

Anakin Skywalker first steps to the Dark Side because of the love he has for his own wife. He is afraid he will lose her so he grabs power and gain. It seems so good and it leads to darkness.

Many legends and stories tell of selling one's soul to the Devil in order to gain something that seems so good. It seems the Devil always shows up demanding the promised soul in return. Jesus says it this way, "What does it do for you to gain the whole world and lose your soul?"

Our text today from James says that what gets us in trouble does not come from without, it comes from within

> Where do all the fights and quarrels among you come from? They come from your desires for pleasure, which are constantly fighting within .You want and you do not have. Your motives are bad. You ask for things for your own pleasure. You are unfaithful and have become a friend of the world and an enemy of God. So submit yourselves to God. Resist the Devil and he will flee.

I do not want to think that the Dark Side has to do with my car, my family, my faith, my nation but the story of God reminds me that is where is starts; with the inordinate emphasis on "mine." The eye of my soul becomes blind to what is my right. I can no longer see the very darkness that is within me.

But the light shines in the darkness. The Devil cannot ultimately win. In fact in the big story the power of evil is already defeated by the victory in Christ. In the old fashioned exorcisms when someone was trying to free an individual from "possession by the Devil," the name of Christ was used over and over again. It seems the Devil cannot stand that name.

The Catholic Church in 1972 discontinued the consecration of "special exorcists." It seems that this did not fit a modern world where the Devil had become out of fashion. Well, today I would remind us that the name of Christ is but the first step in facing the darkness both without and within. To say the name of Christ is only the beginning. The next step is to live the life of Christ and to become peacemakers, liberators of those who are captive, and ones offering new sight to those who are blinded by the powers of evil.

Goodness is stronger than evil, but we must be careful because there is a dark side and it is closer than even next door.

APPENDIX TWELVE

Faith Healing or Healing Faith?

MATTHEW 15:10–28

MAYBE JESUS IS TIRED. After all he finishes telling a whole series of stories that even his closest disciples don't seem to understand. Then he has to come up with enough food to feed 5,000 people. And just before this scene we witness this morning where he calls a desperate woman a dog, Jesus ends up having to rescue his "leader of the pack" from drowning in a sea of doubt.

Good old Simon Peter tries to walk on water only to learn that he is not ready to walk on dry land much less water when it comes to following this new Messiah who will require most everything Peter's got. Maybe Jesus is tired from all of this?

Come on, you explain why Jesus would look down into the eyes of a woman who is pleading for the liberation of her child from disease and call her a dog. Biblical scholars have been trying to sanitize this story every since it was written down a couple of thousand years ago.

One explanation is that the words used for "dog" is *kynarion* which means a household dog rather than the word, *kyon* which means "stray or wild dog." Come on Jesus, this story is still not good for business.

Here I am preaching about how wonderfully inclusive you are, how loving you are, how you love people no matter what and now you call a pleading mother a "dog"; okay a nice dog. What gives here?

I think Jesus is tired. What do you think? Maybe you want to clean this up today because you do not want Jesus to be tired. Jesus is not supposed to get tired. Jesus is our faith hero, bigger than life, divine beyond measure. He can't get tired!

Okay, lets' say that Jesus knows exactly what he is doing. Does this mean that he is simply is a prejudiced leader who knows that salvation is for the elect of God? This woman is a pagan who worships the gods of Phoenicia. She is not a churchgoer and after all she has already exhausted all the faith healers up the road in an attempt to find a cure for her daughter. Jesus is simply her last resort. She does not buy this new faith he offers. She is simply a mother at the end of her rope, but she does not have the proper faith credentials. She is on the list of those considered "outside" the faith.

You know, we have our list do we not? Everybody's list is different. The radical Muslims exclude all non-believers, the radical Christians exclude the Muslims. The religious right excludes those who espouse evolution or the practice of homosexuality, while the left makes everyone who disagrees with them uneducated simpletons.

I do not pretend to understand what is in the mind of Jesus as he looks down into this "outsiders" eyes. We could make this real religious and say that he is simply setting things up so Jody Seymour could preach a sermon generations later. Jesus does not really mean that this poor woman is a dog. He is framing a situation in order to get people's attention.

The trouble is some people in the crowd that day probably want to give Jesus a high five and shout "alleluia." Finally Jesus comes around and sees that those outsiders are unclean and will water down the real faith. The list makers from both sides are happy with Jesus' exclusion of this unclean woman. At last Jesus sees that God ordains that some people should be kept in their place and should keep to their own. Jesus comes around to "sitting in the back of the bus" and separate water fountains for "colored" folks He sees that it is proper and even God ordained.

I would rather think Jesus is tired than to think he is doing this excluding based upon the before mentioned thinking. There is a scene in "Jesus Christ Superstar" where the unwashed masses surround Jesus. The crowd forms a kind of human spider web. Jesus is engulfed in the web. He tries to reach out and touch the mob but they almost consume him and he finally screams out, "Leave me alone, there's too little of me. Heal yourselves."

In the history of doctrine within the Christian tradition when believers get close to a "tired" Jesus we shore him up by adding a bit more divinity to the mixture. Jesus becomes a "high octane" Jesus, powerful beyond the weakness of humanity. When this is done I believe we start to lose the real, incarnate Jesus. Sometimes maybe we need a tired Jesus who shares our humanity.

This not so tired kind of Jesus becomes capable of being the center of what one writer calls "toxic faith." Toxic faith is when religion becomes more important than God. Rules become more important than health. Reality is blurred by a divine God who dictates who is in and who is out. When this happens "faith" needs some healing.

Let's not clean up the story today. Let's let it be. I think Jesus might be tired. He looks down at this woman and offers the company line that he is taught as a child in the synagogue. The Messiah is to first come to the lost sheep of Israel. Gentiles and especially the mongrel Canaanites who have intermarried and polluted the faith are a mixed breed . . . so yes, they are dogs.

This may sound harsh but no harsher than the days when women were second-class, or blacks were slaves as the bible says it should be. Who do you want to put on the outsider list and then justify it with a few verses of scripture?

Maybe Jesus has a plan to get the house of Israel in order first and then he will work on the outsiders, or maybe he is just tired. He uncharacteristically tells this woman, who is crying out to him, to wait in line like a puppy waiting for the family meal to be over.

But are you ready for this? This woman saves Jesus from himself. The mysterious mixture of the human Jesus and the divine Jesus is slapped upside the head with a woman who gives Jesus the opportunity to see real faith at his footsteps.

"It is fair to take the children's food and throw it to the dogs?" Jesus tells the pleading woman. She does not miss a beat. She sees her opening. The disciples are saying to themselves, "Okay maybe now she gets the picture and will leave us alone so we can all go rest."

But no, she is a mother. All mothers listening today understand what she does next. She has a ready-made arsenal of love to fight a battle with this foreign faith healer. She has a child wallowing in misery down the road who needs her to convince this seemingly mean spirited faith healer to give her some morsels from his bag of tricks. She is a heat-seeking missile who will not be deterred by any insult from this religious leader. Her love for her hurting daughter is bigger than her pride. She cares not what he calls her. She wants justice for her child.

She looks up into Jesus' tired face from her kneeling position. The word used in the text means that the position she is in is the same as one takes when kneeling for worship. She pleads, "Okay, okay but listen. Do not people call you 'Lord' and if you are Lord then you are the "Master" of the house, and if you are the Master of the house then listen to me. Even hungry dogs might get a few crumbs from their master's table."

Then there is a moment of silence that we need to feel just now. Stop in this moment for I believe that is what Jesus does. The very tired, human Jesus looks down into her face and for a moment I do not believe he says anything. The world waits, the universe waits, and we wait with the woman for an answer. She is bargaining with Jesus for life. Who will be on the list of outsiders?

I remember bargaining with and for Jesus. I was walking the streets of the old city of Jerusalem. My group was getting ahead of me. Our guide was trying to get us to a shop where I knew he would give us time to buy some of the olive wood figurines that are so famous in the Holy Land.

But the shop that the guide would take us to would have a mark up because the guide always gets a portion of the take. I was told by someone who knew the ropes to slip into one of the other shops and bargain for what I wanted. I am not much of a bargainer but such bargaining is expected in the Middle East. It is a way of life.

"How much is that crucifix," I asked the owner who was busy talking to a friend behind the counter. "$100," he shouted back. I turned to leave. After all my group was getting ahead of me and it is easy to get lost in Jerusalem. "Wait," he shouted, "Where are you going? How much, how much," he shouted.

I was not used to this. After all was I to bargain for Jesus? He came out the door after me. "How much?" I was embarrassed. "Uh, $45," I said. "$45 for Jesus?" he responded. I tried to walk away. He grabbed me, "$50," he said.

I looked down the street. I could no longer see my group. I was going to get lost trying to bargain for Jesus! I reached into my pocket and pulled out two twenties and a ten. He already had the very Jesus in his hand I had pointed to. He shoved the crucifix in my hand and took my money.

Here he is. (I hold up the large wooden crucifix) I bargained for Jesus. It was the thing to do. This woman bargained "with" Jesus. She knows it was the thing to do. It is actually customary to bargain for something in Jesus day and even today in that land called "Holy."

Jesus is brought back to himself by her bargaining. He looks down into her eyes. Knowing Jesus like I do, after all I bought him, he's mine; or is it that he bought me? I am his? Anyway, this tired Jesus is saved from his tiredness by a woman's faith.

I think he might reach down and touch her for she has sure touched him. Coming out of his tired state he tells her that her faith is great. It's not like the disciples' faith, a faith that does not know how to feed the people. It's not like Peter's faith that earlier sinks beneath waves of doubt. This faith is a persistent faith; a faith in spite of things not because of things.

It is not a toxic kind of faith like those religious leaders who just a few moments before read Jesus the riot act because his disciples are eating without the ritual performance of washing their hands. This faith is real, earthy, and yes, dog-like. She may have been called a dog but her bite is one that holds on to what she wants.

Jesus says for the entire world to hear something like, "O my God, what was I thinking. It's been a long day. My dear woman you are the kind of person I long to touch. You are who I have been sent to save. Thank you for saving me from my tiredness with your faith. Go find your daughter and tell her what kind of mother she has, and by the way your faith has healed her. And for all of you who overhear this story and who are caught up in a toxic religiosity that blinds you to the outsiders, let your faith be healed."

Jesus remembers what he has come to live and die for. His tiredness melts away from his weary eyes and he looks down at a woman of great faith. Just a few moments earlier he tells his disciples that it is not the rules and religion that saves a person but the change of heart that must come from within.

This outsider to the faith is a person of great heart. In this magical, mystical, moment for all time Jesus comes into her heart and her life. She gets to Jesus with her faith and Jesus gets to her heart with his faith. It is a faith healing but it is even more a healing of faith. Faith must begin with something that changes our hearts. It is not a matter of ritual or rules. It is something very deep that affects how we see others, how we spend our time and money, and how we order our lives.

Appendix Thirteen

Families, Children, and Teenagers

PROVERBS 6:20–23 / EPHESIANS 5:28–6:4

THIS IS EITHER THE oldest joke in the world or a joke about the oldest issue in the world: Whenever your kids are out of control, you can take comfort from the thought that even God's omnipotence did not extend to God's kids. After creating Heaven and earth, God created Adam and Eve. And the first thing He said to them was:

"Don't."

"Don't what?" Adam replied.

"Don't eat the forbidden fruit," God said.

"Forbidden fruit? We got forbidden fruit? Hey, Eve . . . we got Forbidden Fruit!"

"No way!"

"Yes WAY!"

"Don't eat that fruit!" said God.

"Why?"

"Because I'm your Creator and I said so!" said God, wondering why he hadn't stopped after making the elephants.

A few minutes later God saw the kids having an apple break and was angry. "Didn't I tell you not to eat that fruit?" God asked.

"Uh huh," Adam replied.

"Then why did you?"

"I dunno," Eve answered.

"She started it!" Adam said.

"Did Not!" "DID so!"

"DID NOT!!" Having had it with the two of them, God's punishment was that Adam and Eve should have children of their own.

My mother's way of saying the above is what I call "the most useless words in the English language." She would say to me when I would challenge why she punished me, "You will never understand until you have children of your own." Of course these words are true but their truth must wait for the event to happen to know they are true so why say them?

I stand before you today to say to you that the hardest thing I ever did is not in my work as a pastor. The most challenging thing I have ever done is to be the parent of two teenage daughters.

Standing in the shower at 4:00 o'clock one Sunday morning when I had again caught one of our daughters sneaking out late Saturday night I prayed, "Dear God, I know you can't do much because after all this is a teenage girl and you are only God. I know it is too much to expect you to be able to control her but could you please make her start doing this madness on Friday nights instead of Saturday nights and early Sunday morning? I mean I have to work on Sunday, remember?"

A few weeks later I caught Amanda again but it was Friday night. As I picked her up to haul her back home to be grounded even more, I was laughing. "What are you laughing about," she shouted. I said, "I got my prayer answered." "Don't give me any of that religious mess," she angrily replied. "O don't get me wrong. I did not ask God to make you change because I don't think even God can do anything with you. I just asked that you do this junk on Friday night instead of Saturday, and it's Friday!!"

I selected two passages of scripture for today that deal with family and parenting so in case you do not agree with what I say in this sermon I want you to at least hear what the bible says about family, children, and parents. The mutual respect between husband and wife is commanded in the scripture. It is not optional. To mistreat each other within the covenant of marriage is a violation against God. It's that simple.

The image of the body of Christ is used as an analogy of husband and wife. Marriage is that important. It is the reason we stand before God at an altar to say our vows. I have told you many times that God loves us but God does not trust us. The joke that begins the sermon has a ring of truth in it. We are disobedient children who seek our own pleasure even in our marriages so we make vows in front of God and witnesses so that when we walk by forbidden fruit and it looks tempting we at least have rings and vows to help us remember how weak and selfish we can be.

Children are reminded to obey their parents and parents are reminded to instruct and discipline children. This is also not optional. When one of our teenage daughters screamed into my face, "Who are you to tell me what to do?" I tried to get her to at least hear me say the following:

> Buried in a jar somewhere is a sacred scroll. On that scroll are words, which say something like this: For a few brief years I get to tell you what to do. I am the parent and you are not. Someday you might be a parent and you will get to tell your children what do to. You do not have to like it and you do not have to agree with it. I might even be wrong, but I am your parent and you have to struggle to do what I ask of you. It will not be long before you will be out of this house and you will get to do what you please without me around. Until that point the rule of the universe is that I am the parent and you are not.

The Bible backs this up. It is true that some parents forfeit their parental rights by being abusive parents. God makes exceptions for abuse but abuse is defined as extreme physical or psychological mistreatment. Allowing children to rule in the family unit is another form of abuse. Such giving over of authority to children is not part of God's plan, it is also emotionally unhealthy and it is not smart.

Good parenting is authoritative not authoritarian. God put it in the contract that we are to discipline and instruct children. To not do so is to forfeit our end of the bargain. And yes, if you are a child or teenager and you are here today because you heard that I am giving you the chance to defend yourself after this sermon, you need to know that if you are baptized we promised God that we would raise you in the church.

This is also not optional. You do not have to buy or accept our concept of God but until you leave home we promised God that we would expose you to this faith. If you think it is boring I am sorry. I really do not want it to be boring but some good things have a boring element to them. Sit-ups are boring but they make your flabby, perhaps pierced or tattooed belly firm.

Psychologists have studied teenage behavior and have discovered that teenage boredom comes from not liking something or not being able to handle it. We at least are supposed to expose you to the reality that you are a child of God. You do not remember being born but we remember it and we believe that you were given to us by God. You are a gift.

The Christian faith is valuable to us and we hope it will be valuable to you. If it is not valuable to you right now and even if it is boring we want to expose you to it because we believe that some of it will sink in even if you do not like it or if some of it makes you uncomfortable. One day you can choose what to do with this faith but if we don't let you know about it you will not even be able to say no to it intelligently. We promised God we would do this. It's that simple, and besides you might as well learn now that some things in life will be boring at first but good later on.

I have also discovered that there is a difference between what parents want and what children and teenagers want. Kids have more dreams than reality while parents have more reality than dreams. Independence is the risk for kids while letting go is the risk for parents. We parents want to invest in our children while our children want to invest in their peers.

I also learned the hard way as a parent what one psychologist portrays as the 4 cardinal sins of parenting are true: 1) spontaneous problem discussions do not usually work; 2) nagging is not very productive; 3) insight transplants do not work; and 4) arguing is pointless.

So to combat this we need to find time to discuss difficult issues rather than trying to handle them in the heat of battle. Nagging is futile even if it feels natural. I cannot give you my values the best I can do is model them and offer them to you. And sometimes I will walk away from an argument and simply tell you that this is the way it is. If you want to discuss it rationally I will listen but it does not mean that I will agree or give in.

Parents need to not major in the minors. Some battles are not worth fighting but some are. Core values are not negotiable. Messy rooms and what you wear might be discussion points. Underage drinking, sex before you are ready, rude language and behavior, consistent lying, and your basic health are not negotiable no matter how wrong or crazy you think we are. Remember the scroll in that jar. It's the rules and you will not or should not understand until you have children of your own and you are not there yet but we are, and believe me and us "It ain't easy."

So here is my sermon for parents based on what I've learned and read.

ᴄᴠ Do not give up your role. You are the parent. Do not be a tyrant but be firm and authoritative. Your kids do not have to like you. You are not their buddy. If they do not like you now most of the time they will come around later. Do not take their bad feelings for you personally. (And by the way if any of you kids out there are still listening, we parents have feelings too and they can be hurt because we really do love you and the old song, "You always hurt the one you love" is true)

∾ Do not give up on your child but you may have to do what I had to do and learn the difference between giving up and letting go. Give freedom but remind them that freedom when it comes to the family is earned and can be lost. That is the way real life is and your task is to introduce them to real life not sheltered life with no consequences. (The biggest parenting mistake I made was not frustrating my children enough and not allowing them to hurt a bit more by paying for the consequences of their actions. My protection of them felt like love but it was really a form of codependency. I was protecting myself too and it did not do them long term good. Life has consequences and overprotection and shielding is not real love)

∾ Ask God to help you have faith in the long term. This is the short term and kids will not always be teenagers. Pray for patience while you stand firm. Be willing to listen to expectations but that does not mean you have to agree or give in. Try to focus on character not just behavior. Failing to do something that is agreed upon is not just about breaking some rule it is about trust.

I asked our Pastoral Counselor John Rowe to offer some thoughts based on what he sees in his work with families. John offers two basic thoughts. Consumerism has invaded the family so that families think they have to be the all everything family with the all everything products and do the all everything life thus filling up all available time with everything. Relationships get lost in the pace. Relationships are still fundamental.

Second, what we forgot in our family of origin gets remembered in our own family and if we are not careful we project some form of it onto our family. Self-work is important so that we will not try to "make up" for what we did not get in our family of origin.

Thich Nhat Hanh the monk who shares wonderful wisdom says this:

> Look closely at the palm of your hand and you will see your parents and all the generations of your ancestors. All of them are alive at this moment. Each is present in your body. You are a continuation of these people.

But since we are spiritual creatures and are not just animals that perform instinctual, set behaviors we can develop self-reflection and we can change. We do not have to repeat the unhealthy patterns that we learned in the past.

Here is a poem that when I first read it seemed to me to be the stupidest thing I had ever heard. After being a parent and living and learning I discovered its wisdom.

ON CHILDREN

by Kahil Gibran

Your children are not your children
They are sons and daughters of Life's longing for itself
They come through you but not from you
And though they are with you yet they belong not to you
You may give them your love but not your thoughts
For they have their own thoughts
You can house their bodies but not their souls
For their souls dwell in the house of tomorrow
A place you cannot visit, not even in your dreams
You may strive to be like them,
But seek not to make them like you
For life goes not backward nor can tarries with yesterday
You are bows from which your children
As living arrows are sent forth
The archer sets the mark upon the path of the infinite
And he bends you with his might
That His arrows may go swift and far.
Let your bending in the archer's hand be for gladness
For even as He loves the arrow that flies
So He loves also the bow that is stable.[1]

Here is what I have learned from scripture, from 38 years of marriage, and from parenting:

∾ Husbands love your wives and wives love your husbands. Love changes and feelings subside. Every marriage has cracks in it but light can come through the cracks. Work on your marriage if it is still intact. You promised God that you would work on your marriage when you stood at an altar long ago and said words whose meaning you did not realize. God

---

1. Gibran, *The Prophet*, 17.

knew you would have trouble in your marriage that is why you made the promises. God will always love you but God really does not trust you/us.

∾ Marriage takes priority over the kids. It may not seem like that should be true but if you do not work on your marriage when the cracks start forming, and they will form when you have kids and especially when they are very young and when they are teenagers, you will pay a price and so will your kids. Work on the marriage first. It is a way of loving your kids.

∾ For a while kids have to obey parents. They do not have to agree with you or even like you. Yes, you have feelings too but do not put them so up front especially with teenagers. Remember how selfish and self absorbed you were when you were a teenager. By the rules of the universe and God's rules you are the parent and you are to be an authoritative parent. Yes, you will be wrong sometimes, and yes you will need to deeply listen to your children and not write them off but do not give them the parenting role even if they want it. It's not right and it will hurt them in the long run. Freedom is earned and should be denied when promises are broken. Make consequences equivalent to the broken promises. Arguing and nagging are useless. You cannot make your children have your values no matter how many "insight transplants" you attempt. The best you can do is model your values and show them they are important to you even if they are not important to them. Believe me, more sinks in that you think even when they throw it back at you with anger and misunderstanding. Some of it sticks to their hands when they throw it and some of it sinks into their souls even though they do not know it. It will come out later to your surprise and maybe even theirs.

∾ We are spiritual beings and so are children. Your religion may not be relevant to your children and may even seem boring. God is still God and we are all gifts of God. Somewhere sometime your children will discover that spiritual things are important, maybe not now. But you promised God when God gave you the kids and when you brought them to baptism that you would expose them to the value of faith. There was no vow that said they had to like it. Some really good things are hard things. If coming to church at least half of the time with you is hard then at least you are keeping your vows. Trust God that they might get something that they can use later to make their own decisions about their own faith. Don't give up because they give you grief.

∾ And if you are a child/teenager and you are awake right now, You have no idea how much God loves you. In moments that you do not understand your parents and in moments when you do not understand yourself but may be afraid to say it, God really knows you. You are God's even if you do not think God is around. If you have a hard time believing in God, get in line with a bunch of young people who are experiencing the strange land between childhood faith and the faith needed in adulthood. You are not there yet and it may seem like the wilderness because you can't buy into what your parents believe. Well, believe it or not this wilderness has a place in your later faith so hang in there even when you have trouble believing because God always believes in you and longs to be there to help you.

   ∾ And lastly, think of the long term. Never give up on relationships. Be careful of making life so full of activities and things that you cover up relationships that need attention. Being uncomfortable is part of growth. God knew this from the very beginning when God said, "Hey kids, Adam, Eve don't" and we "did." But God never, never gives up on us.

Bibliography

Arlen, Harold. *The Wizard of Oz, If I Were King of the Forest,* Audio CD, MGM, 1995.

Bourgeault, Cynthia. *Cynthia Bourgeault: Silence Is God's First Language,* No pages. 2004. Online: http//www.beliefnet.com/Faiths/Faith-Tools/Medication/2004/11/Silence-Is-Gods-First-Language.aspx.

Buffett, Jimmy. *Take the Weather with You. Breathe In, Breathe Out, Move On.* Audio CD, RCA, 2006.

Carpenter, Mary Chapin. *Passionate Kisses,* Audio CD, Columbia, 1992.

Cohen, Leonard. *Essential Leonard Cohen, Anthem,* Audio CD, Sony, 2002.

Covey, Stephen R., et al. *First Things First: To Live, To Love, To Learn, To Leave a Legacy,* New York: Simon & Schuster, 1994.

Dylan, Bob. *Gotta Serve Somebody: The Gospel Songs of Bob Dylan, Gotta Serve Somebody,* Audio CD, Sbme Special Mkts, 2003.

Elliott, T. S. *Four Quartets,* New York: Harcourt, Brace and Company, 1943.

Gibran, Kahlil. *The Prophet.* New York, Knopf, 1968.

Haas, David. *The Faith We Sing, You Are Mine,* Abingdon Press, Nashville, 2000. 2218.

Healey, Joseph G. *Once Upon a Time in Africa: Stories of Wisdom and Joy,* Maryknoll, New York: Orbis Books, 2004.

Jacobs, Gregg D. *The Ancestral Mind: Reclaim the Power,* New York: Viking, 2003.

Lesser, Elizabeth. *New American Spirituality: A Seekers Guide,* New York: Random House, 1999.

Long, Thomas G. *Surprise Party, The Christian Century,* 2001. Online: http://www.testweek.com/mtlk/lk15/htm.

McGowen, Brian. *Marginally Mark,* by and Anglican priest in Western Australia. No pages. 2008. Online: http//www.textweek.com/mkjnacts/mark1b.htm.

Miller, Timothy, Ph. D., *How to Want What You Have: Discovering the Magic and Grandeur of Ordinary Existence,* 1st ed. New York: H. Holt, 1995.

Morrow, Lance. *Evil an Investigation.* New York, NY: Basic Books, 2003.

Muller, Wayne. *Sabbath: Restoring the Sacred Rhythm of Rest,* New York: Bantam Books, 1999.

Nanus, Burt. *Visionary Leadership: Creating a Compelling Sense of Director for Your Organization,* 1st ed. San Francisco: Jossey-Bass, 1992.

Nepo, Mark, *The Exquisite Risk: Daring to Live an Authentic Life,* 1st ed. New York: Harmony Books, 2005.

Nouwen, Henri J. M. *The Return of the Prodigal Son: A Story of Homecoming,* New York: Continuum, 1995.

Paterson, Stephen, et al., *The Gospel of Thomas,* The Gnostic Society Library, 2009. Online: http://www.gnosis.org/naghamm/nhl_thomas.htm.

Pearsall, Paul, Ph.D. *The Pleasure Principal: To Love, To Work, To Play—Life in the Balance,* 1st ed. Alameda, CA: Hunter House Publishers, 1996.

Restak, Richard M., M.D. *The New Brain: How the Modern Age Is Rewiring Your Mind,* Emmaus, PA: Rodale Press, 2003.

Remen, Rachel Naomi. *My Grandfather's Blessings: Stories of Strength, Refuge, and Belonging,* New York: Riverhead Books, 2000.

Smith, Christian, with Melinda Lundquist Denton, *Soul Searching: The Religious and Spiritual Lives of American Teenagers,* New York: Oxford University Press, 2005.

Staub, Dick. *The Culturally Savvy Christian: A Manifesto for Deepening Faith and Enriching Popular Culture in an Age of Christianity-Lite,* 1st ed. San Francisco, CA: Jossey-Bass, 2007.

Warren, Richard. *The Purpose-Driven Life: What on Earth am I here for?* Grand Rapids, MI: Zondervan, 2002.